D0439417

THE BOOK OF
GREAT AMERICAN
DOCUMENTS

Edited, with Introductions by
VINCENT WILSON, JR.

American History Research Associates
Silver Spring, Maryland

Copyright © 1967 by American History Research Associates
All rights reserved.

LIBRARY OF CONGRESS CATALOG CARD No. 67-28440

Printed in the United States of America

by

Judd & Detweiler, Inc.
Washington, D.C.

American History Research Associates
20 SHAW AVE., SILVER SPRING, MARYLAND

Contents

Introduction

The Declaration of Independence—the Constitution—the Bill of Rights—the Gettysburg Address—these are documents that every American knows instinctively are an important part of his heritage. But just what do they mean? What is their significance to Americans today?

The texts of these and other great documents are here presented with introductions that seek to discover their enduring significance and the meaning they have for Americans in the twentieth century.

These documents chart the progress of man's quest for freedom on this continent, and of his monumental achievement in building and maintaining a free society. The United States of America was the first nation of the world created by the pen as well as the sword; and the ideas expressed in these documents have shaped the lives of all Americans: indeed, these ideas, perhaps more than the vast, rich continent and the American people themselves, have given America its unique identity among the nations of history.

Faith in the rightness of these ideas has come down through the years from the Founding Fathers. The signers of the Declaration had faith enough in the "self-evident" truths to pledge their lives, their fortunes, and their sacred honor. And the framers of the Constitution had faith enough in the ideas in that document to make a constitution, for the first time in history, the supreme law of the land. In these and the other documents presented here are the spirit and essence of our political heritage, but today these documents are more often worshipped than understood.

This book is meant to be *read*. It includes photographs of all of the original documents that are available, but each of the documents is also published in large, readable type, so that the citizen, young or old, may not merely possess, but read and know, understand and cherish.

The Fundamental Orders

1639

"The first written constitution known to history that created a government, and it marked the beginning of American democracy."

—JOHN FISKE

On January 14, 1639, planters from the small towns of Hartford, Wethersfield, and Windsor, meeting in a special convention at Hartford, adopted the Fundamental Orders to "associate and conjoin [themselves] to be as one Public State or Commonwealth." Nineteen years after the Mayflower landed at Plymouth, these men created the first written constitution that set permanent limitations on governmental power, that established a representative system of government, and that provided the right to vote to all free men. By adopting it as the form of government for their commonwealth, they also became the first to create a new government embodying democratic principles.

Particularly significant is the absence, in the Fundamental Orders, of any reference to England or the authority of the Crown or Parliament. In the wilderness along the Connecticut River, the three towns had, in fact, come close to creating an independent commonwealth.

Most of the ideas incorporated in the Fundamental Orders came from the Reverend Thomas Hooker, who in 1636 had led about one hundred of his congregation from Cambridge, Massachusetts, into the wilderness, finally to settle on the Connecticut River at what is now Hartford. He left Cambridge for the same reason he had left England several years before: a learned and daring scholar-preacher, he had fearlessly advocated what were considered radical views on both religious and political liberty. He fled England to

5

escape arrest for his preaching; he left Massachusetts because he did not agree with the authorities on a number of political issues, especially their belief that the right to vote should be restricted to church members. In 1638, in a sermon at Hartford, he laid down the principles that proved to be the foundation of democratic government in Connecticut.

But the Fundamental Orders gave the world more than the basic principles of democratic and representative government: they introduced a unique political relationship between the towns and the commonwealth they created, a pattern for sharing the responsibilities of governing that was later closely followed by other States and that, in 1787, was seized by the framers of the U.S. Constitution as the solution to the problem of the union of the States—the federal system. Thus, the principle at the heart of the American Union may be traced to the document that established the union of the three tiny, primitive towns in the Connecticut valley almost 150 years before that famous convention met in Philadelphia.

FORASMUCH as it hath pleased the Almighty God by the wise disposition of his divine providence so to order and dispose of things that we the Inhabitants and Residents of Windsor, Hartford, and Wethersfield are now cohabiting and dwelling in and upon the River of Connectecotte and the lands thereunto adjoining; and well knowing where a people are gathered together the word of God requires that to maintain the peace and union of such a people there should be an orderly and decent Government established according to God, to order and dispose of the affairs of the people at all seasons as occasion shall require; do therefore associate and conjoin ourselves to be as one Public State or Commonwealth; and do for ourselves and our Successors and such as shall be adjoined to us at any time hereafter, enter into Combination and Confederation together, to maintain and preserve the liberty and purity of the Gospel of our Lord Jesus which we now profess, as also, the discipline of the Churches, which according to the truth of the said Gospel is now practiced amongst us; as also in our Civil affairs to be guided and governed according to such Laws, Rules, Orders, and Decrees as shall be made, ordered, and decreed as followeth:—

1. It is Ordered, sentenced, and decreed, that there shall be yearly two General Assemblies or Courts, the one the second Thursday in April, the other the second Thursday in September following; the first shall be called the Court of Election, wherein shall be yearly chosen from time to time, so many Magistrates and other public Officers as shall be found requisite: Whereof one to be chosen Governor for the year ensuing and until another be chosen, and no other Magistrate to be chosen for more than one year: provided always there be six chosen besides the Governor, which being chosen and sworn according to an Oath recorded for that purpose, shall have power to administer justice according to the Laws here established, and for want thereof, according to the rule of the Word of God; which choice shall be made by all that are admitted freemen and have taken the Oath of Fidelity, and do cohabit within this Jurisdiction (*Having been admitted Inhabitants by the major part of the Town wherein they live) or the major part of such as shall be then present.

2. It is Ordered, sentenced, and decreed, that the Election of the aforesaid Magistrates shall be on this manner: every person present and qualified for choice shall bring in (to the persons deputed to receive them) one single paper with the name of him written in it whom he desires to have Governor, and he that hath the greatest number of papers shall be Governor for that year. And the rest of the Magistrates or public officers to be chosen in this manner: the Secretary for the time being shall first read the names of all that are to be put to choice and then shall severally nominate them distinctly, and every one that would have the person nominated to be chosen shall bring in one single paper written upon, and he that would not have him chosen shall bring in a blank; and every one that hath more written papers than blanks shall be a Magistrate for that year; which papers shall be received and told by one or more that shall be then chosen by the court and sworn to be faithful therein; but in case there should not be six chosen as aforesaid, besides the Governor, out of those which are nominated, then he or they which have the most written papers shall be a Magistrate or Magistrates for the ensuing year, to make up the aforesaid number.

---

*This clause was interlined in a different handwriting, and is of a later date. It was adopted by the General Court of November, 1643.

3. It is Ordered, sentenced, and decreed, that the Secretary shall not nominate any person, nor shall any person be chosen newly into the Magistracy which was not propounded in some General Court before, to be nominated the next Election; and to that end it shall be lawful for each of the Towns aforesaid by their deputies to nominate any two whom they conceive fit to be put to election; and the Court may add so many more as they judge requisite.

4. It is Ordered, sentenced, and decreed, that no person be chosen Governor above once in two years, and that the Governor be always a member of some approved congregation, and formerly of the Magistracy within this Jurisdiction; and all the Magistrates, Freemen of this Commonwealth; and that no Magistrate or other public officer shall execute any part of his or their office before they are severally sworn, which shall be done in the face of the court if they be present, and in case of absence by some deputed for that purpose.

5. It is Ordered, sentenced, and decreed, that to the aforesaid Court of Election the several Towns shall send their deputies, and when the Elections are ended they may proceed in any public service as at other Courts. Also the other General Court in September shall be for making of laws, and any other public occasion, which concerns the good of the Commonwealth.

6. It is Ordered, sentenced, and decreed, that the Governor shall, either by himself or by the Secretary, send out summons to the Constables of every Town for the calling of these two standing Courts one month at least before their several times: And also if the Governor and the greatest part of the Magistrates see cause upon any special occasion to call a General Court, they may give order to the Secretary so to do within fourteen days' warning: and if urgent necessity so required, upon a shorter notice, giving sufficient grounds for it to the deputies when they meet, or else be questioned for the same; And if the Governor and major part of Magistrates shall either neglect or refuse to call the two General standing Courts or either of them, as also at other times when the occasions of the Commonwealth require, the Freemen thereof, or the major part of them, shall petition to them so to do; if then it be either denied or neglected, the said Freemen, or the major part of them, shall have power to give order to the Constables of the several Towns to do the same, and so may meet together, and choose to themselves a Moderator, and may proceed to do any act of power which any other General Courts may.

7. It is Ordered, sentenced, and decreed, that after there are warrants given out for any of the said General Courts, the Constable or Constables of each Town, shall forthwith give notice distinctly to the inhabitants of the same, in some public assembly or by going or sending from house to house, that at a place and time by him or them limited and set, they meet and assemble themselves together to elect and choose certain deputies to be at the General Court then following to agitate the affairs of the Commonwealth; which said deputies shall be chosen by all that are admitted Inhabitants in the several Towns and have taken the oath of fidelity; provided that none be chosen a Deputy for any General Court which is not a Freeman of this Commonwealth.

The aforesaid deputies shall be chosen in manner following: every person that is present and qualified as before expressed, shall bring the names of such, written in several papers, as they desire to have chosen for that employment, and these three or four, more or less, being the number agreed on to be chosen for that time, that have greatest number of papers written for them shall be deputies for that Court; whose names shall be endorsed on the back side of the warrant and returned into the Court, with the constable or constables' hand unto the same.

8. It is Ordered, sentenced, and decreed, that Windsor, Hartford, and Wethersfield shall have power, each Town, to send four of their Freemen as their deputies to every General Court; and Whatsoever other Town shall be hereafter added to this Jurisdiction, they shall send so many deputies as the Court shall judge meet, a reasonable proportion to the number of Freemen that are in the said Towns being to be attended therein; which deputies shall have the power of the whole Town to give their votes and allowance to all such laws and orders as may be for the public good, and unto which the said Towns are to be bound.

9. It is Ordered and decreed, that the deputies thus chosen shall have power and liberty to appoint a time and a place of meeting together before any General Court, to advise and consult of all such things as may concern the good of the public, as also to examine their own Elections, whether according to the order, and if they or the greatest part of them find any election to be illegal they may seclude such for present from their meeting, and return the same and their reasons to the Court; and if it prove true, the Court may fine the party or parties so intruding, and the Town, if they see cause, and give out a warrant to go to a new election in a

legal way, either in part or in whole. Also the said deputies shall have power to fine any that shall be disorderly at their meetings, or for not coming in due time or place according to appointment; and they may return the said fines into the Court if it be refused to be paid, and the Treasurer to take notice of it, and to escheat or levy the same as he does other fines.

10. It is Ordered, sentenced, and decreed, that every General Court, except such as through neglect of the Governor and the greatest part of Magistrates the Freemen themselves do call, shall consist of the Governor, or some one chosen to moderate the Court, and four other Magistrates at least, with the major part of the deputies of the several Towns legally chosen; and in case the Freemen, or major part of them, through neglect or refusal of the Governor and major part of the Magistrates, shall call a Court, it shall consist of the major part of Freemen that are present or their deputies, with a Moderator chosen by them: In which said General Courts shall consist the supreme power of the Common-wealth, and they only shall have power to make laws or repeal them, to grant levies, to admit of Freemen, dispose of lands un-disposed of, to several Towns or persons, and also shall have power to call either Court or Magistrate or any other person whatsoever into question for any misdemeanor, and may for just causes dis-place or deal otherwise according to the nature of the offense; and also may deal in any other matter that concerns the good of this Commonwealth, except election of Magistrates, which shall be done by the whole body of Freemen.

In which Court the Governor or Moderator shall have power to order the Court, to give liberty of speech, and silence unseasonable and disorderly speakings, to put all things to vote, and in case the vote be equal to have the casting voice. But none of these Courts shall be adjourned or dissolved without the consent of the major part of the Court.

11. It is Ordered, sentenced, and decreed, that when any General Court upon the occasions of the Commonwealth have agreed upon any sum, or sums of money to be levied upon the several Towns within this Jurisdiction, that a committee be chosen to set out and appoint what shall be the proportion of every Town to pay of the said levy, provided the committee be made up of an equal number out of each Town.

14th January 1639 the 11 Orders above said are voted.

The Declaration of Independence
Thomas Jefferson
1776

"Yesterday the greatest question was decided which ever was debated in America; and a greater perhaps never was, nor will be, decided among men. A resolution was passed without one dissenting colony, that those United Colonies are, and of right ought to be, free and independent States."

—JOHN ADAMS

On June 7, 1776, Richard Henry Lee of Virginia introduced to the Continental Congress the resolution that "these United Colonies are, and of right ought to be, free and independent States." For years the idea of independence had been spreading among the colonists; it gained force in the 1760's, when Britain, freed from the French and Indian War, turned her attention to the rich trade with the American colonies.

By its restrictive policies toward American commerce, Britain was able to maintain a favorable balance of trade—obtaining raw materials cheaply from the colonies and selling back to the colonies the goods she manufactured. But, caught up in its long war with France (1754-1763), Britain had been lax in trying to enforce these policies, and the American traders had become accustomed to the freedom of direct trade with other countries. Thus the colonists were in no mood to accept the stringent tax laws passed by the Parliament—the Sugar Act (1764), Stamp Act (1765), and the famous Tea Act (1773). The Stamp Act—requiring tax stamps on newspapers, magazines and other documents—was particularly distasteful, and colonists flatly denounced it, showing such re-

11

THE NATIONAL ARCHIVES

Engrossed Declaration of Independence

sistance that it was finally repealed. But these taxes—coupled with the King's declaring the colonists rebels, and such writings as Thomas Paine's Common Sense—gradually led many colonists to lend a sympathetic ear to the revolutionary cries of the more extreme patriotic groups that had sprung up, such as the Sons of Liberty.

The author of several revolutionary pamphlets, Thomas Paine had sensed better than most what a rare opportunity the colonists had before them. He was the one who helped them think in terms of a continent, their continent, with room enough for a large dream. And Thomas Jefferson was the man with the great gift that enabled him to put that dream into the immortal words of the Declaration.

Written in June of 1776, in the week after Lee had introduced his resolution for independence, the Declaration was almost solely the product of Jefferson's pen. As chairman of the committee appointed by Congress to draw up a statement, Jefferson wrote the initial draft. Two members of the committee—Benjamin Franklin and John Adams—inserted a few changes, and Congress later made a few more, but it is, in effect, the work of Jefferson, and some of his most distinctive qualities—his devotion to justice and his faith in ideas—shine through many of its lines.

Designed to present the Americans' case to the tribunal of the world, the Declaration appeals to the common sense and reason of mankind, in order to win favor and support. The Preamble has often been cited as a great political and a great human statement: the greatness is not so much in the principles that are there boldly set forth as in the simple fact that this represented the first time in history that these principles were being put into action, as the basis for founding a new government and a new nation. Jefferson and the other signers of the Declaration took the giant step of making the ideal real. That is why this document stands as one of the truly great facts of human history: in one sudden thrust, man vaulted to an entirely new level of political life, and a kind of freedom that before had been only a matter of philosophical discussion was now a political goal to the achievement of which these founders of a new nation had most solemnly committed their "lives, fortunes and [their] sacred honor."

A Declaration by the Representatives of the UNITED STATES OF AMERICA, in General Congress assembled.

When in the course of human events it becomes necessary for one people to dissolve the political bands which have connected them with another, and to assume among the powers of the earth the separate and equal station to which the laws of nature & of nature's god entitle them, a decent respect to the opinions of mankind requires that they should declare the causes which impel them to the separation.

We hold these truths to be self-evident; that all men are created equal & independent, that from that equal creation they derive rights inherent & inalienable, among which are the preservation of life, & liberty, & the pursuit of happiness; that to secure these rights, governments are instituted among men, deriving their just powers from the consent of the governed: that whenever any form of government becomes destructive of these ends, it is the right of the people to alter or to abolish it, & to institute new government, laying it's foundation on such principles & organising it's powers in such form, as to them shall seem most likely to effect their safety & happiness. prudence indeed will dictate that governments long established should not be changed for light & transient causes: and accordingly all experience hath shewn that mankind are more disposed to suffer while evils are sufferable, than to right themselves by abolishing the forms to which they are accustomed. but when a long train of abuses & usurpations [begun at a distinguished period & pursuing invariably the same object, evinces a design to reduce them under absolute Despotism, it is their right, it is their duty, to throw off such government & to provide new guards for their future security. such has been the patient sufferance of these colonies; & such is now the necessity which constrains them to expunge their former systems of government. the history of the present king of Great Britain is a history of unremitting injuries and usurpations, among which appears no solitary fact to contradict the uniform tenor of the rest all of which have in direct object the establishment of an absolute tyranny over these states. to prove this, let facts be submitted to a candid world, for the truth of which we pledge a faith yet unsullied by falsehood.

LIBRARY OF CONGRESS

Jefferson's Draft of the Declaration

By their action, the men who signed the Declaration, for the first time in history, made revolution an instrument that could be used by honorable men for a just cause. And the Declaration has inspired and influenced free men on every continent in the years since. Perhaps more than any other single document, the Declaration represents the great watershed in the political history of man: at that dramatic moment in the summer of 1776 when the Declaration was passed, the ageless tyranny of despotic rule was, at one blow, formally denounced and broken. The echo of that blow will surely ring down through the ages.

WHEN IN THE COURSE of human events it becomes necessary for one people to dissolve the political bands which have connected them with another, and to assume among the powers of the earth, the separate and equal station to which the Laws of Nature and of Nature's God entitle them, a decent respect to the opinions of mankind requires that they should declare the causes which impel them to the separation.

We hold these truths to be self-evident, that all men are created equal, that they are endowed by their Creator with certain unalienable rights, that among these are life, liberty and the pursuit of happiness. That to secure these rights, governments are instituted among men, deriving their just powers from the consent of the governed. That whenever any form of government becomes destructive of these ends, it is the right of the people to alter or to abolish it, and to institute new government, laying its foundation on such principles and organizing its powers in such form, as to them shall seem most likely to effect their safety and happiness. Prudence, indeed, will dictate that governments long established should not be changed for light and transient causes; and accordingly all experience hath shown, that mankind are more disposed to suffer, while evils are sufferable, than to right themselves by abolishing the forms to which they are accustomed. But when a long train of abuses and usurpations, pursuing invariably the same object, evinces a design to reduce them under absolute despotism, it is their right, it is their duty, to throw off such government, and to provide new guards for

15

their future security. Such has been the patient sufferance of these Colonies; and such is now the necessity which constrains them to alter their former systems of government. The history of the present King of Great Britain is a history of repeated injuries and usurpations, all having, in direct object, the establishment of an absolute tyranny over these States. To prove this, let facts be submitted to a candid world.

He has refused his assent to laws, the most wholesome and necessary for the public good.

He has forbidden his Governors to pass laws of immediate and pressing importance, unless suspended in their operation till his assent should be obtained; and when so suspended, he has utterly neglected to attend to them.

He has refused to pass other laws for the accommodation of large districts of people, unless those people would relinquish the right of representation in the legislature, a right inestimable to them and formidable to tyrants only.

He has called together legislative bodies at places unusual, uncomfortable, and distant from the depository of their public records, for the sole purpose of fatiguing them into compliance with his measures.

He has dissolved representative houses repeatedly, for opposing with manly firmness his invasions on the rights of the people.

He has refused for a long time, after such dissolutions, to cause others to be elected; whereby the legislative powers, incapable of annihilation, have returned to the people at large for their exercise; the State remaining in the meantime exposed to all the dangers of invasion from without and convulsions within.

He has endeavoured to prevent the population of these states; for that purpose obstructing the laws of naturalization of foreigners; refusing to pass others to encourage their migration hither, and raising the conditions of new appropriations of lands.

He has obstructed the administration of justice, by refusing his assent to laws for establishing judiciary powers.

He has made judges dependent on his will alone, for the tenure of their offices, and the amount and payment of their salaries.

He has erected a multitude of new offices, and sent hither swarms of officers to harass our people, and eat out their substance.

He has kept among us, in times of peace, standing armies without the consent of our legislatures.

He has affected to render the military independent of, and superior to, the civil power.

He has combined with others to subject us to a jurisdiction foreign to our constitution, and unacknowledged by our laws; giving his assent to their acts of pretended legislation:

For quartering large bodies of armed troops among us:

For protecting them, by a mock trial, from punishment for any murders which they should commit on the inhabitants of these States:

For cutting off our trade with all parts of the world:

For imposing taxes on us without our consent:

For depriving us, in many cases, of the benefits of trial by jury:

For transporting us beyond seas to be tried for pretended offences:

For abolishing the free system of English laws in a neighbouring Province, establishing therein an arbitrary government, and enlarging its boundaries so as to render it at once an example and fit instrument for introducing the same absolute rule into these Colonies:

For taking away our Charters, abolishing our most valuable laws, and altering fundamentally the forms of our governments:

For suspending our own legislatures, and declaring themselves invested with power to legislate for us in all cases whatsoever.

He has abdicated government here, by declaring us out of his protection and waging war against us.

He has plundered our seas, ravaged our coasts, burnt our towns, and destroyed the lives of our people.

He is, at this time, transporting large armies of foreign mercenaries to complete the works of death, desolation and tyranny, already begun, with circumstances of cruelty and perfidy scarcely paralleled in the most barbarous ages, and totally unworthy the head of a civilized nation.

He has constrained our fellow citizens taken captive on the high seas to bear arms against their country, to become the executioners of their friends and brethren, or to fall themselves by their hands.

He has excited domestic insurrections amongst us, and has endeavoured to bring on the inhabitants of our frontiers, the merciless Indian savages, whose known rule of warfare is an undistinguished destruction of all ages, sexes, and conditions.

In every stage of these oppressions we have petitioned for redress in the most humble terms: our repeated petitions have been answered only by repeated injury. A prince whose character is thus

17

marked by every act which may define a tyrant is unfit to be the ruler of a free people.

Nor have we been wanting in attention to our British brethren. We have warned them from time to time of attempts by their legislature to extend an unwarrantable jurisdiction over us. We have reminded them of the circumstances of our emigration and settlement here. We have appealed to their native justice and magnanimity, and we have conjured them by the ties of our common kindred to disavow these usurpations, which would inevitably interrupt our connections and correspondence. They too have been deaf to the voice of justice and of consanguinity. We must, therefore, acquiesce in the necessity, which denounces our separation, and hold them, as we hold the rest of mankind, enemies in war, in peace, friends.

We, therefore, the Representatives of the United States of America, in General Congress assembled, appealing to the Supreme Judge of the world for the rectitude of our intentions, do, in the name, and by authority of the good people of these Colonies, solemnly publish and declare, That these United Colonies are, and of right ought to be, Free and Independent States; that they are absolved from all allegiance to the British Crown, and that all political connection between them and the State of Great Britain, is and ought to be totally dissolved; and that as Free and Independent States, they have full power to levy war, conclude peace, contract alliances, establish commerce, and to do all other acts and things which Independent States may of right do. And for the support of this declaration, with a firm reliance on the protection of Divine Providence, we mutually pledge to each other our lives, our fortunes, and our sacred honor.

John Hancock

NEW HAMPSHIRE
Josiah Bartlett
Wm. Whipple
Matthew Thornton

MASSACHUSETTS BAY
Saml. Adams
John Adams
Robt. Treat Paine
Elbridge Gerry

DELAWARE
Caesar Rodney
Geo. Read
Tho. M'Kean

MARYLAND
Samuel Chase
Wm. Paca
Thos. Stone
Charles Carroll of Carrollton

NEW YORK
Wm. Floyd
Phil. Livingston
Frans. Lewis
Lewis Morris

NORTH CAROLINA
Wm. Hooper
Joseph Hewes
John Penn

SOUTH CAROLINA
Edward Rutledge
Thos. Heyward, Junr.
Thomas Lynch, Junr.
Arthur Middleton

NEW JERSEY
Richd. Stockton
Jno. Witherspoon
Fras. Hopkinson
John Hart
Abra. Clark

RHODE ISLAND
Step. Hopkins
William Ellery

CONNECTICUT
Roger Sherman
Sam'el Huntington
Wm. Williams
Oliver Wolcott

GEORGIA
Button Gwinnett
Lyman Hall
Geo. Walton

PENNSYLVANIA
Robt. Morris
Benjamin Rush
Benja. Franklin
John Morton
Geo. Clymer
Jas. Smith
Geo. Taylor
James Wilson
Geo. Ross

VIRGINIA
George Wythe
Richard Henry Lee
Th. Jefferson
Benja. Harrison
Ths. Nelson, Jr.
Francis Lightfoot Lee
Carter Braxton

COURTESY CAPITOL HISTORICAL SOCIETY

The Declaration of Independence. Jefferson presents the document to John Hancock. Painting by John Trumbull.

Resolved

That these United Colonies are, and of right ought to be, free and independent States, that they are absolved from all allegiance to the British Crown, and that all political connection between them and the State of Great Britain is, and ought to be, totally dissolved.

That it is expedient forthwith to take the most effectual measures for forming foreign Alliances.

That a plan of confederation be prepared and transmitted to the respective Colonies for their consideration and approbation.

THE NATIONAL ARCHIVES

Lee Resolution for Independence, June 7, 1776

The Northwest Ordinance

1787

"We are accustomed to praise the lawgivers of antiquity; we help to perpetuate the fame of Solon and Lycurgus; but I doubt whether one single law of any lawgiver, ancient or modern, has produced effects of more distinct, marked, and lasting character than the Ordinance of 1787."

—DANIEL WEBSTER

The Northwest Ordinance, or the Ordinance of 1787, was a simple yet generous solution to the political problem posed by the lands west of the Alleghenies and northwest of the Ohio River called the Northwest Territory, a vast wilderness that was part of the land won from the British. Largely through the efforts of Thomas Jefferson, the States from Massachusetts to Virginia had agreed to relinquish their claims to this land, leaving the Continental Congress responsible for the newly formed territory.

The Ordinance of 1787 was the most important act passed by the Continental Congress, which struggled under the weak Articles of Confederation from 1781 until 1789, when the Constitution established a new government. The Ordinance guaranteed that inhabitants of the territory would have the same rights and privileges that citizens of the thirteen States enjoyed, but the most important features of the Ordinance were Articles 5 and 6, which provided a formula for making new States and prohibited the practice of slavery in the territory. Jefferson had written both of these into an ordinance he had drafted in 1784, but the article on slavery had been rejected by a single vote, and the 1784 ordinance had never been put in effect. But finally, on July 13, 1787, the document presented here was passed by Congress.

Important as it was that slavery was prohibited in this virgin land —for it set the pattern for the western territories, it is the provision

21

An ORDINANCE for the GOVERNMENT of the TERRITO-RY of the UNITED STATES, North-West of the RIVER OHIO.

BE IT ORDAINED by the United States in Congress assembled, That the said territory, for the purposes of temporary government, be one district; subject, however, to be divided into two districts, as future circumstances may, in the opinion of Congress, make it expedient.

It is hereby ordained and declared by the authority aforesaid, That the following articles shall be considered as articles of compact between the original states and the people and states in the said territory, and forever remain unalterable, unless by common consent, to wit:

Article the First. No person, demeaning himself in a peaceable and orderly manner, shall ever be molested on account of his mode of worship or religious sentiments in the said territory.

Article the Second. The inhabitants of the said territory shall always be entitled to the benefits of the writ of habeas corpus, and of the trial by jury; of a proportionate representation of the people in the legislature, and of judicial proceedings according to the course of the common law; all persons shall be bailable unless for capital offences, where the proof shall be evident, or the presumption great; all fines shall be moderate, and no cruel or unusual punishments shall be inflicted; no man shall be deprived of his liberty or property but by the judgment of his peers, or the law of the land; and should the public exigencies make it necessary for the common preservation to take any person's property, or to demand his particular services, full compensation shall be made for the same;— and in the just preservation of rights and property it is understood and declared, that no law ought ever to be made, or have force in the said territory, that shall in any manner whatever interfere with, or affect private contracts or engagements, bona fide and without fraud previously formed.

Article the Third. Religion, morality and knowledge, being necessary to good government and the happiness of mankind, schools and the means of education shall forever be encouraged. The utmost good faith shall always be observed towards the Indians; their lands and property shall never be taken from them without their consent; and in their property, rights and liberty, they never shall be invaded or disturbed, unless in just and lawful wars authorised by Congress; but laws founded in justice and humanity shall from time to time be made, for preventing wrongs being done to them, and for preserving peace and friendship with them.

Article the Fourth. The said territory, and the states which may be formed therein, shall forever remain a part of this confederacy of the United States of America, subject to the articles of confederation, and to such alterations therein as shall be constitutionally made; and to all the acts and ordinances of the United states in Congress assembled, conformable thereto. The inhabitants and settlers in the said territory, shall be subject to pay a part of the federal debts contracted or to be contracted, and a proportional part of the expences of government, to be apportioned on them by Congress, according to the same common rule and measure by which apportionments thereof shall be made on the other states; and the taxes for paying their proportion, shall be laid and levied by the authority and direction of the legislatures of the district or districts or new states, as in the original states, within the time agreed upon by the United States in Congress assembled. The legislatures of those districts, or new states, shall never interfere with the primary disposal of the soil by the United States in Congress assembled, nor with any regulations Congress may find necessary for securing the title in such soil to the bona fide purchasers. No tax shall be imposed on lands the property of the United States; and in no case shall non-resident proprietors be taxed higher than residents. The navigable waters leading into the Mississippi and St. Lawrence, and the carrying places between the same shall be common highways, and forever free, as well to the inhabitants of the said territory, as to the citizens of the United States, and those of any other states that may be admitted into the confederacy, without any tax, impost or duty therefor.

Article the Fifth. There shall be formed in the said territory, not less than three nor more than five states; and the boundaries of the states, as soon as Virginia shall alter her act of cession and consent to the same, shall become fixed and established as follows, to wit: The western state in the said territory, shall be bounded by the Mississippi, the Ohio and Wabash rivers; a direct line drawn from the Wabash and Post Vincent's due north to the territorial line between the United States and Canada, and by the said territorial line to the lake of the Woods and Mississippi. The middle state shall be bounded by the said direct line, the Wabash from Post Vincent's to the Ohio; by the Ohio, by a direct line drawn due north from the mouth of the Great Miami to the said territorial line, and by the said territorial line. The eastern state shall be bounded by the last mentioned direct line, the Ohio, Pennsylvania, and the said territorial line: Provided however, and it is further understood and declared, that the boundaries of these three states, shall be subject so far to be altered, that if Congress shall hereafter find it expedient, they shall have authority to form one or two states in that part of the said territory which lies north of an east and west line drawn through the southerly bend or extreme of lake Michigan: and whenever any of the said states shall have sixty thousand free inhabitants therein, such state shall be admitted by its delegates into the Congress of the United states, on an equal footing with the original states in all respects whatever; and shall be at liberty to form a permanent constitution and state government: Provided the constitution and government so to be formed, shall be republican, and in conformity to the principles contained in these articles; and so far as it can be consistent with the general interest of the confederacy, such admission shall be allowed at an earlier period, and when there may be a less number of free inhabitants in the state than sixty thousand.

Article the Sixth. There shall be neither slavery nor involuntary servitude in the said territory, otherwise than in punishment of crimes whereof the party shall have been duly convicted: Provided always, that any person escaping into the same, from whom labor or service is lawfully claimed in any one of the original states, such fugitive may be lawfully reclaimed and conveyed to the person claiming his or her labor or service as aforesaid.

Be it ordained by the authority aforesaid, That the resolutions of the 23d of April, 1784, relative to the subject of this ordinance, be, and the same are hereby repealed and declared null and void.

DONE by the UNITED STATES in CONGRESS assembled, the 13th day of July, in the year of our Lord 1787, and of their sovereignty and independence the 12th.

THE NATIONAL ARCHIVES

The Northwest Ordinance

for the forming of new States, in Article 5, that makes the Northwest Ordinance one of the great documents in American history. These are the key words: ".... whenever any of the said States shall have 60,000 free inhabitants therein, such State shall be admitted, by its delegates, into the Congress of the United States, on an equal footing with the original States in all respects whatever...."

Throughout history, nations acquiring new or undeveloped lands had generally kept those territories—and their peoples—in a distinctly subordinate role. It was indeed revolutionary for the powerful established States—Virginia, New York, Pennsylvania, Massachusetts, and the rest—to say, in effect, to the people west of the Alleghenies: "Settle the land and form your own territorial government. When you have accomplished this, and grown sufficiently, you may apply to take your place among us—not as a colony, not as a protectorate or dependency, but as an absolute equal, as another State." And this great principle, once established, extended to the other territories the United States acquired; it became the principle that made it possible for the small collection of new States spread out along the Atlantic coast to grow across the entire continent and, in recent years, even across the waters to Hawaii. Here the truth that the Declaration of Independence asserted to be self-evident, "that all men are created equal," was given substance and life, and for the first time in history a political document was created that dared to offer the status and dignity of equality to people in states yet unformed. Here, indeed, was an enlightened moment in American history.

BE IT ORDAINED by the United States in Congress assembled, That the said territory, for the purposes of temporary government, be one district, subject, however, to be divided into two districts, as future circumstances may, in the opinion of Congress, make it expedient. . . .

It is hereby ordained and declared by the authority aforesaid, That the following articles shall be considered as articles of compact between the original States and the people and States in the said territory and forever remain unalterable, unless by common consent, to wit:

Art. 1st. No person, demeaning himself in a peaceable and orderly manner, shall ever be molested on account of his mode of worship or religious sentiments, in the said territory.

Art. 2d. The inhabitants of the said territory shall always be entitled to the benefits of the writ of *habeas corpus,* and of the trial by jury; of a proportionate representation of the people in the legislature; and of judicial proceedings according to the course of the common law. All persons shall be bailable, unless for capital offences, where the proof shall be evident or the presumption great. All fines shall be moderate; and no cruel or unusual punishments shall be inflicted. No man shall be deprived of his liberty or property, but by the judgment of his peers or the law of the land; and, should the public exigencies make it necessary, for the common preservation, to take any person's property, or to demand his particular services, full compensation shall be made for the same. And, in the just preservation of rights and property, it is understood and declared, that no law ought ever to be made, or have force in the said territory, that shall, in any manner whatever, interfere with or affect private contracts or engagements, *bona fide*, and without fraud, previously formed.

Art. 3d. Religion, morality, and knowledge, being necessary to good government and the happiness of mankind, schools and the means of education shall forever be encouraged. The utmost good faith shall always be observed towards the Indians; their lands and property shall never be taken from them without their consent; and, in their property, rights, and liberty, they shall never be invaded or disturbed, unless in just and lawful wars authorized by Congress; but laws founded in justice and humanity, shall, from time to time, be made for preventing wrongs being done to them, and for preserving peace and friendship with them.

Art. 4th. The said territory, and the States which may be formed therein, shall forever remain a part of this confederacy of the United States of America, subject to the Articles of Confederation, and to such alterations therein as shall be constitutionally made; and to all the acts and ordinances of the United States in Congress assembled, conformable thereto. The inhabitants and settlers in the said territory shall be subject to pay a part of the federal debts contracted or to be contracted, and a proportional part of the expenses of government, to be apportioned on them by Congress according to the same common rule and measure by which apportionments thereof shall be made on the other States; and the taxes, for paying their proportion, shall be laid and levied by the authority and direction of the legislatures of the district or districts, or new States, as in the original States, within the time agreed upon by the United States in Congress assembled. The legislatures of those districts or new States, shall never interfere with the primary disposal of the soil by the United States in Congress assembled, nor with any regulations Congress may find necessary for securing the title in such soil to the *bona fide* purchasers. No tax shall be imposed on lands the property of the United States; and, in no case, shall non-resident proprietors be taxed higher than residents. The navigable waters leading into the Mississippi and St. Lawrence, and the carrying places between the same, shall be common highways, and forever free, as well to the inhabitants of the said territory as to the citizens of the United States, and those of any other States that may be admitted into the Confederacy, without any tax, impost, or duty, therefor.

Art. 5th. There shall be formed in the said territory, not less than three nor more than five States. . . . And, whenever any of the said States shall have 60,000 free inhabitants therein, such State shall be admitted, by its delegates, into the Congress of the United States, on an equal footing with the original States in all respects whatever, and shall be at liberty to form a permanent constitution and State government: *Provided,* the constitution and government so to be formed, shall be republican, and in conformity to the principles contained in these articles; and, so far as it can be consistent with the general interest of the confederacy, such admission shall be allowed at an earlier period, and when there may be a less number of free inhabitants in the State than 60,000.

Art. 6th. There shall be neither slavery nor involuntary servitude in the said territory, otherwise than in the punishment of crimes, whereof the party shall have been duly convicted: *Provided, always,* That any person escaping into the same, from whom labor or service is lawfully claimed in any one of the original States, such fugitive may be lawfully reclaimed and conveyed to the person claiming his or her labor or service as aforesaid.

Be it ordained by the authority aforesaid, That the resolutions of the 23d of April, 1784, relative to the subject of this ordinance, be, and the same are hereby, repealed and declared null and void.

Done by the United States, in Congress assembled, the 13th day of July, in the year of our Lord 1787, and of their sovereignty and independence the twelfth.

COURTESY NATIONAL PARK SERVICE

Restored Assembly Room, Independence Hall.
The Declaration of Independence was adopted and the Constitution was written here.

26

The Constitution of the United States
1787

"The example of changing a constitution, by assembling the wise men of the State, instead of assembling armies, will be worth as much to the world as former examples we have given them. The Constitution . . . is unquestionably the wisest ever yet presented to men."

—THOMAS JEFFERSON

The first words of the Preamble of the Constitution—"We, the people of the United States, . . . do ordain and establish. . ."—were, in 1787, almost as revolutionary as the Revolutionary War itself. Here for the first time the radical idea of the political theorists that a government rests upon the consent *of the people was, by a stroke of the pen, made a political fact: in this new government, the authority to establish a constitution did, without question, come from the people. The framers of the Constitution began the Preamble by simply confirming the idea of popular sovereignty that Thomas Jefferson, in the Declaration of Independence, had proclaimed to be self-evident: that governments derive "their just powers from the consent of the governed." But the framers of the Constitution did far more: they produced a document that solved a remarkable number of the political problems that had plagued men and nations throughout history, a document that John Adams called —and history has proved—"the greatest single effort of national deliberation that the world has ever seen."*

In 1786, three years after the Revolutionary War had ended, thoughtful men in most of the independent States had become concerned about the failures of their improvised system of government. It had become apparent that the Articles of Confederation, which had often proved weak and ineffective during the war years, were

THE NATIONAL ARCHIVES

First page of the engrossed Constitution of the United States.

proving to be even weaker and less effective in time of peace. After the victory, the relations between individual States began to worsen; petty quarrels increased as each State jealously asserted its independence and its interests. Unless some more successful system of central government could be devised, there was a real danger that the Confederation might eventually be dissolved, leaving thirteen struggling sovereign States, each driven by fear and suspicion to raise its own army, defend its borders, and ultimately be doomed to re-enact the bloody history of the European states.

The Articles of Confederation linked the States in a "firm league of friendship with each other," according to Article III, but these Articles, which had been drawn up during the war under the shadow of British tyranny, provided for a "government" that had none of the powers necessary to govern. They provided no permanent executive and no federal judiciary, only a single body—Congress, in which each of the sovereign States had one vote. And Congress had no real power: it could not tax, raise armies or pay debts; it could simply requisition the States for funds, and, in war, for arms and men. The weakness of this system—the sovereign States often simply refused to honor the requisitions—had given Washington some of his darkest moments during the war. And, after the war, since Congress had no power to regulate commerce between States, some States passed tariff laws against each other and issued paper money, currency that could be used only within their own borders. States quarreled over boundaries, and one (New Jersey) had its own customs service.

Washington had early seen the weakness of the Articles of Confederation, but it was Alexander Hamilton, his aide-de-camp during the war, who probably did more than any other man to bring delegates from the States together to consider the problem. He wrote a series of newspaper articles, and, in 1782, offered a proposal to Congress, suggesting that a convention be held. In 1786 he represented New York at a meeting held at Annapolis to consider commercial regulations governing navigation of Chesapeake Bay and the Potomac. Although all the States had been invited, only five were represented, and by far the most important result of the meeting was the report, written by Hamilton, that recommended to Congress that all the States send delegates to a convention in Philadelphia to consider "the trade and commerce of the United States."

A *cautious* Congress called the convention for the "sole and express purpose of revising the Articles of Confederation," and in May of 1787 fifty-five delegates from twelve States (all but Rhode Island) met at the State House (now Independence Hall) in Philadelphia to begin deliberations. Washington was the permanent chairman. Seventy-year-old Benjamin Franklin provided the wisdom and reasonableness that saw the convention through a number of crises. Jefferson and Adams, both in Europe representing their country, followed the progress of the convention and offered encouragement through the painfully slow mail packets. James Madison, Alexander Hamilton, George Mason, James Wilson and Gouverneur Morris contributed most to the document that the convention produced in mid-September of that year. As it developed, they did not merely revise the Articles of Confederation; they devised an entirely new plan, one that was agreed upon only after four months of strenuous, often bitter, debate.

The Articles of Confederation had been designed to preserve each State's sovereignty, but this "league of friendship" between States had failed. And what must rank as the greatest achievement of the members of the convention was their solution of this problem: they made the Constitution the supreme law of the land, and they made it derive its powers from ("We, the people of the United States . . ."), and for the most part operate on, the people, not the States. To find their answer, the delegates had gone to the constitutions of many of the States—to the principle of federation first delineated in the Fundamental Orders of Connecticut.

In solving this and other political problems, the delegates at the convention in Philadelphia did far more than make the first formally written constitution: they also performed the awesome task of making a new nation.

COURTESY CAPITOL HISTORICAL SOCIETY

Scene at the signing of the Constitution of the United States. Painting by Howard Chandler Christy.

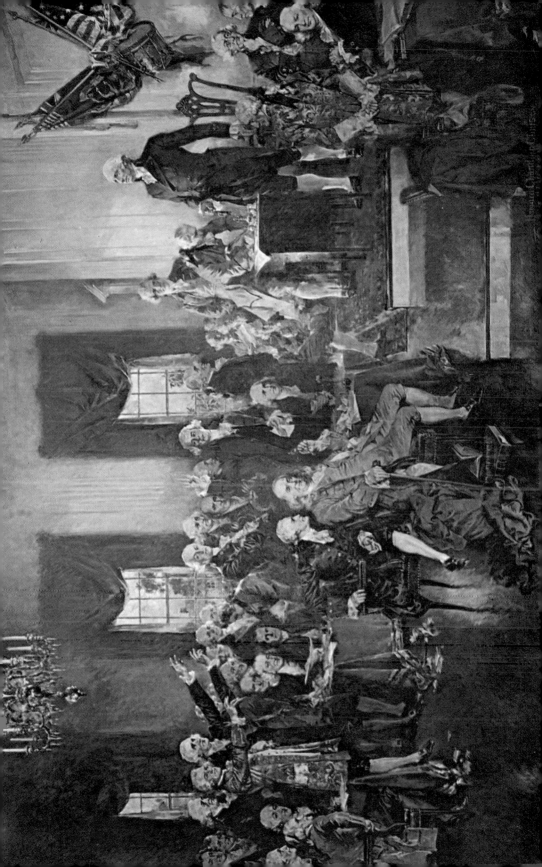

WE, THE PEOPLE of the United States, in order to form a more perfect union, establish justice, insure domestic tranquility, provide for the common defense, promote the general welfare, and secure the blessings of liberty to ourselves and our posterity, do ordain and establish this Constitution for the United States of America.

ARTICLE I

Section 1. All legislative powers herein granted shall be vested in a Congress of the United States, which shall consist of a Senate and House of Representatives.

Section 2. 1. The House of Representatives shall be composed of members chosen every second year by the people of the several States, and the electors in each State shall have the qualifications requisite for electors of the most numerous branch of the State legislature.

2. No person shall be a representative who shall not have attained to the age of twenty-five years, and been seven years a citizen of the United States, and who shall not, when elected, be an inhabitant of that State in which he shall be chosen.

3. Representatives and direct taxes shall be apportioned among the several States which may be included within this Union, according to their respective numbers, which shall be determined by adding to the whole number of free persons, including those bound to service for a term of years, and excluding Indians not taxed, *three fifths of all other persons.* The actual enumeration shall be made within three years after the first meeting of the Congress of the United States, and within every subsequent term of ten years, in such manner as they shall by law direct. The number of representatives shall not exceed one for every thirty thousand, but each State shall have at least one representative; and until such enumeration shall be made, the State of New Hampshire shall be entitled to choose three, Massachusetts eight, Rhode Island and Providence Plantations one, Connecticut five, New York six, New Jersey four, Pennsylvania eight, Delaware one, Maryland six, Virginia ten, North Carolina five, South Carolina five, and Georgia three.

4. When vacancies happen in the representation from any State, the executive authority thereof shall issue writs of election to fill such vacancies.

5. The House of Representatives shall choose their speaker and other officers; and shall have the sole power of impeachment.

Section 3. 1. The Senate of the United States shall be composed of two senators from each State, *chosen by the legislature thereof,* for six years; and each senator shall have one vote.

2. Immediately after they shall be assembled in consequence of the first election, they shall be divided as equally as may be into three classes. The seats of the senators of the first class shall be vacated at the expiration of the second year, of the second class at the expiration of the fourth year, and of the third class at the expiration of the sixth year, so that one third may be chosen every second year; and if vacancies happen by resignation, or otherwise, during the recess of the legislature of any State, the executive thereof may make temporary appointments until the next meeting of the legislature, which shall then fill such vacancies.

3. No person shall be a senator who shall not have attained to the age of thirty years, and been nine years a citizen of the United States, and who shall not, when elected, be an inhabitant of that State for which he shall be chosen.

4. The Vice-President of the United States shall be President of the Senate, but shall have no vote, unless they be equally divided.

5. The Senate shall choose their other officers, and also a president *pro tempore,* in the absence of the Vice-President, or when he shall exercise the office of the President of the United States.

6. The Senate shall have the sole power to try all impeachments. When sitting for that purpose, they shall be on oath or affirmation. When the President of the United States is tried, the chief justice shall preside: and no person shall be convicted without the concurrence of two thirds of the members present.

7. Judgment in cases of impeachment shall not extend further than to removal from office, and disqualifications to hold and enjoy any office of honor, trust or profit under the United States: but the party convicted shall nevertheless be liable and subject to indictment, trial, judgment and punishment, according to law.

Section 4. 1. The times, places, and manner of holding elections for senators and representatives, shall be prescribed in each state by the legislature thereof; but the Congress may at any time by law make or alter such regulations, except as to the places of choosing senators.

2. The Congress shall assemble at least once in every year, and such meeting shall be on the first Monday in December, unless they shall by law appoint a different day.

Section 5. 1. Each House shall be the judge of the elections, returns and qualifications of its own members, and a majority of each shall constitute a quorum to do business; but a smaller number may adjourn from day to day, and may be authorized to compel the attendance of absent members, in such manner, and under such penalties as each House may provide.

2. Each House may determine the rules of its proceedings, punish its members for disorderly behavior, and, with the concurrence of two thirds, expel a member.

3. Each House shall keep a journal of its proceedings, and from time to time publish the same, excepting such parts as may in their judgment require secrecy; and the yeas and nays of the members of either House on any question shall, at the desire of one fifth of those present, be entered on the journal.

4. Neither House, during the session of Congress, shall, without the consent of the other, adjourn for more than three days, nor to any other place than that in which the two Houses shall be sitting.

Section 6. 1. The senators and representatives shall receive a compensation for their services, to be ascertained by law, and paid out of the Treasury of the United States. They shall in all cases, except treason, felony, and breach of the peace, be privileged from arrest during their attendance at the session of their respective Houses, and in going to and returning from the same; and for any speech or debate in either House, they shall not be questioned in any other place.

2. No senator or representative shall, during the time for which he was elected, be appointed to any civil office under the authority of the United States, which shall have been created, or the emoluments whereof shall have been increased during such time; and no person holding any office under the United States shall be a member of either House during his continuance in office.

Section 7. 1. All bills for raising revenue shall originate in the House of Representatives; but the Senate may propose or concur with amendments as on other bills.

2. Every bill which shall have passed the House of Representatives and the Senate, shall, before it becomes a law, be presented to the President of the United States; if he approve he shall sign it, but if not he shall return it, with his objections, to that House in which it shall have originated, who shall enter the objections at

large on their journal, and proceed to reconsider it. If after such reconsideration two thirds of that House shall agree to pass the bill, it shall be sent, together with the objections, to the other House, by which it shall likewise be reconsidered, and if approved by two thirds of that House, it shall become a law. But in all such cases the votes of both Houses shall be determined by yeas and nays, and the names of the persons voting for and against the bill shall be entered on the journal of each House respectively. If any bill shall not be returned by the President within ten days (Sundays excepted) after it shall have been presented to him, the same shall be a law, in like manner as if he had signed it, unless the Congress by their adjournment prevent its return, in which case it shall not be a law.

3. Every order, resolution, or vote to which the concurrence of the Senate and the House of Representatives may be necessary (except on a question of adjournment) shall be presented to the President of the United States; and before the same shall take effect, shall be approved by him, or being disapproved by him, shall be repassed by two thirds of the Senate and House of Representatives, according to the rules and limitations prescribed in the case of a bill.

Section 8. The Congress shall have the power

1. To lay and collect taxes, duties, imposts, and excises, to pay the debts and provide for the common defense and general welfare of the United States; but all duties, imposts, and excises shall be uniform throughout the United States;

2. To borrow money on the credit of the United States;

3. To regulate commerce with foreign nations, and among the several States, and with the Indian tribes;

4. To establish a uniform rule of naturalization, and uniform laws on the subject of bankruptcies throughout the United States;

5. To coin money, regulate the value thereof, and of foreign coin, and fix the standard of weights and measures;

6. To provide for the punishment of counterfeiting the securities and current coin of the United States;

7. To establish post offices and post roads;

8. To promote the progress of science and useful arts, by securing for limited times to authors and inventors the exclusive right to their respective writings and discoveries;

9. To constitute tribunals inferior to the Supreme Court;

10. To define and punish piracies and felonies committed on the high seas, and offenses against the law of nations;

11. To declare war, grant letters of marque and reprisal, and make rules concerning captures on land and water;

12. To raise and support armies, but no appropriation of money to that use shall be for a longer term than two years;

13. To provide and maintain a navy;

14. To make rules for the government and regulation of the land and naval forces;

15. To provide for calling forth the militia to execute the laws of the Union, suppress insurrections and repel invasions;

16. To provide for organizing, arming, and disciplining the militia, and for governing such part of them as may be employed in the service of the United States, reserving to the States respectively, the appointment of the officers, and the authority of training the militia according to the discipline prescribed by Congress;

17. To exercise exclusive legislation in all cases whatsoever, over such district (not exceeding ten miles square) as may, by cession of particular States, and the acceptance of Congress, become the seat of the government of the United States, and to exercise like authority over all places purchased by the consent of the legislature of the State in which the same shall be, for the erection of forts, magazines, arsenals, dockyards, and other needful buildings; and

18. To make all laws which shall be necessary and proper for carrying into execution the foregoing powers, and all other powers vested by this Constitution in the government of the United States, or in any department or officer thereof.

Section 9. 1. The migration or importation of such persons as any of the States now existing shall think proper to admit, shall not be prohibited by the Congress prior to the year one thousand eight hundred and eight, but a tax or duty may be imposed on such importation, not exceeding ten dollars for each person.

2. The privilege of the writ of *habeas corpus* shall not be suspended, unless when in cases of rebellion or invasion the public safety may require it.

3. No bill of attainder or *ex post facto* law shall be passed.

4. No capitation, or other direct, tax shall be laid, unless in proportion to the census or enumeration hereinbefore directed to be taken.

5. No tax or duty shall be laid on articles exported from any State.

6. No preference shall be given by any regulation of commerce or revenue to the ports of one State over those of another: nor shall vessels bound to, or from, one State be obliged to enter, clear, or pay duties in another.

7. No money shall be drawn from the treasury, but in consequence of appropriations made by law; and a regular statement and account of the receipts and expenditures of all public money shall be published from time to time.

8. No title of nobility shall be granted by the United States: and no person holding any office of profit or trust under them, shall, without the consent of the Congress, accept of any present, emolument, office, or title, of any kind whatever, from any king, prince, or foreign State.

Section 10. 1. No State shall enter into any treaty, alliance, or confederation; grant letters of marque and reprisal; coin money; emit bills of credit; make anything but gold and silver coin a tender in payment of debts; pass any bill of attainder, *ex post facto* law, or law impairing the obligation of contracts, or grant any title of nobility.

2. No State shall, without the consent of the Congress, lay any imposts or duties on imports or exports, except what may be absolutely necessary for executing its inspection laws; and the net produce of all duties and imposts laid by any State on imports or exports, shall be for the use of the Treasury of the United States; and all such laws shall be subject to the revision and control of the Congress.

3. No State shall, without the consent of the Congress, lay any duty of tonnage, keep troops, or ships of war in time of peace, enter into any agreement or compact with another State, or with a foreign power, or engage in war, unless actually invaded, or in such imminent danger as will not admit of delay.

ARTICLE II

Section 1. 1. The executive power shall be vested in a President of the United States of America. He shall hold his office during the term of four years, and, together with the Vice President, chosen for the same term, be elected as follows:

2. Each State shall appoint, in such manner as the legislature thereof may direct, a number of electors, equal to the whole number of senators and representatives to which the State may be entitled in the Congress: but no senator or representative, or person holding an office of trust or profit under the United States, shall be ap-appointed an elector.

The electors shall meet in their respective States, and vote by ballot for two persons, of whom one at least shall not be an in-habitant of the same State with themselves. And they shall make a list of all the persons voted for, and of the number of votes for each; which list they shall sign and certify, and transmit sealed to the seat of the government of the United States, directed to the President of the Senate. The President of the Senate shall, in the presence of the Senate and House of Representatives, open all the certificates, and the votes shall then be counted. The person hav-ing the greatest number of votes shall be the President, if such number be a majority of the whole number of electors appointed; and if there be more than one who have such majority, and have an equal number of votes, then the House of Representatives shall immediately choose by ballot one of them for President; and if no person have a majority, then from the five highest on the list the said House shall in like manner choose the President. But in choos-ing the President, the votes shall be taken by States, the representa-tion from each State having one vote; a quorum for this purpose shall consist of a member or members from two thirds of the States, and a majority of all the States shall be necessary to a choice. In every case, after the choice of the President, the person having the greatest number of votes of the electors shall be the Vice President. But if there should remain two or more who have equal votes, the Senate shall choose from them by ballot the Vice Presi-dent.

3. The Congress may determine the time of choosing the electors, and the day on which they shall give their votes; which day shall be the same throughout the United States.

4. No person except a natural born citizen, or a citizen of the United States at the time of the adoption of this Constitution, shall be eligible to the office of President; neither shall any person be eligible to that office who shall not have attained to the age of thirty-five years, and been fourteen years a resident within the United States.

5. In case of the removal of the President from office, or of his death, resignation, or inability to discharge the powers and duties of the said office, the same shall devolve on the Vice President, and the Congress may by law provide for the case of removal, death, resignation, or inability, both of the President and Vice President, declaring what officer shall then act as President, and such officer shall act accordingly, until the disability be removed, or a President shall be elected.

6. The President shall, at stated times, receive for his services a compensation, which shall neither be increased nor diminished during the period for which he shall have been elected, and he shall not receive within that period any other emolument from the United States, or any of them.

7. Before he enter on the execution of his office, he shall take the following oath or affirmation:—"I do solemnly swear (or affirm) that I will faithfully execute the office of President of the United States, and will to the best of my ability, preserve, protect and defend the Constitution of the United States."

Section 2. 1. The President shall be Commander-in-chief of the Army and Navy of the United States, and of the militia of the several States, when called into the actual service of the United States; he may require the opinion, in writing, of the principal officer in each of the executive departments, upon any subject relating to the duties of their respective offices, and he shall have power to grant reprieves and pardons for offenses against the United States, except in cases of impeachment.

2. He shall have power, by and with the advice and consent of the Senate, to make treaties, provided two-thirds of the senators present concur; and he shall nominate, and by and with the advice and consent of the Senate, shall appoint ambassadors, other public ministers and consuls, judges of the Supreme Court, and all other officers of the United States, whose appointments are not herein otherwise provided for, and which shall be established by law: but the Congress may by law vest the appointment of such inferior officers, as they think proper, in the President alone, in the courts of law, or in the heads of departments.

3. The President shall have power to fill up all vacancies that may happen during the recess of the Senate, by granting commissions which shall expire at the end of their next session.

Section 3. He shall from time to time give to the Congress information of the state of the Union, and recommend to their consideration such measures as he shall judge necessary and expedient; he may, on extraordinary occasions, convene both Houses, or either of them, and in case of disagreement between them with respect to the time of adjournment, he may adjourn them to such time as he shall think proper; he shall receive ambassadors and other public ministers; he shall take care that the laws be faithfully executed, and shall commission all the officers of the United States.

Section 4. The President, Vice President, and all civil officers of the United States, shall be removed from office on impeachment for, and conviction of, treason, bribery, or other high crimes and misdemeanors.

ARTICLE III

Section 1. The judicial power of the United States shall be vested in one Supreme Court, and in such inferior courts as the Congress may from time to time ordain and establish. The judges, both of the Supreme and inferior courts, shall hold their offices during good behavior, and shall, at stated times, receive for their services, a compensation which shall not be diminished during their continuance in office.

Section 2. 1. The judicial power shall extend to all cases, in law and equity, arising under this Constitution, the laws of the United States, and treaties made, or which shall be made, under their authority;—to all cases affecting ambassadors, other public ministers and consuls;—to all cases of admiralty and maritime jurisdiction;—to controversies to which the United States shall be a party;—to controversies between two or more States;—between a State and citizens of another State;—between citizens of different States;—between citizens of the same State claiming lands under grants of different States, and between a State, or the citizens thereof, and foreign States, citizens or subjects.

2. In all cases affecting ambassadors, other public ministers and consuls, and those in which a State shall be party, the Supreme Court shall have original jurisdiction. In all the other cases before mentioned, the Supreme Court shall have appellate jurisdiction, both as to law and to fact, with such exceptions, and under such regulations as the Congress shall make.

3. The trial of all crimes, except in cases of impeachment, shall be by jury; and such trial shall be held in the State where the said crimes shall have been committed; but when not committed within any State, the trial shall be at such place or places as the Congress may by law have directed.

Section 3. 1. Treason against the United States shall consist only in levying war against them, or in adhering to their enemies, giving them aid and comfort. No person shall be convicted of treason unless on the testimony of two witnesses to the same overt act, or on confession in open court.

2. The Congress shall have power to declare the punishment of treason, but no attainder of treason shall work corruption of blood, or forfeiture except during the life of the person attained.

ARTICLE IV

Section 1. Full faith and credit shall be given in each State to the public acts, records, and judicial proceedings of every other State. And the Congress may by general laws prescribe the manner in which such acts, records and proceedings shall be proved, and the effect thereof.

Section 2. 1. The citizens of each State shall be entitled to all privileges and immunities of citizens in the several States.

2. A person charged in any State with treason, felony, or other crime, who shall flee from justice, and be found in another State, shall, on demand of the executive authority of the State from which he fled, be delivered up to be removed to the State having jurisdiction of the crime.

3. No person held to service or labor in one State under the laws thereof, escaping into another, shall, in consequence of any law or regulation therein, be discharged from such service or labor, but shall be delivered up on claim of the party to whom such service or labor may be due.

Section 3. 1. New States may be admitted by the Congress into this Union; but no new State shall be formed or erected within the jurisdiction of any other State; nor any State be formed by the junction of two or more States, or parts of States, without the consent of the legislatures of the States concerned as well as of the Congress.

2. The Congress shall have power to dispose of and make all needful rules and regulations respecting the territory or other property belonging to the United States; and nothing in this Constitution shall be so construed as to prejudice any claims of the United States, or of any particular State.

Section 4. The United States shall guarantee to every State in this Union a republican form of government, and shall protect each of them against invasion; and on application of the legislature, or of the executive (when the legislature cannot be convened), against domestic violence.

ARTICLE V

The Congress, whenever two thirds of both Houses shall deem it necessary, shall propose amendments to this Constitution, or, on the application of the legislatures of two-thirds of the several States, shall call a convention for proposing amendments, which, in either case, shall be valid to all intents and purposes, as part of this Constitution, when ratified by the legislatures of three-fourths of the several States, or by conventions in three fourths thereof, as the one or the other mode of ratification may be proposed by the Congress; Provided that no amendment which may be made prior to the year one thousand eight hundred and eight shall in any manner affect the first and fourth clauses in the ninth section of the first article; and that no State, without its consent, shall be deprived of its equal suffrage in the Senate.

ARTICLE VI

1. All debts contracted and engagements entered into, before the adoption of this Constitution, shall be as valid against the United States under this Constitution, as under the Confederation.

2. This Constitution, and the laws of the United States which shall be made in pursuance thereof, and all treaties made, or which shall be made, under the authority of the United States, shall be the supreme law of the land; and the Judges in every State shall be bound thereby, anything in the Constitution or laws of any State to the contrary notwithstanding.

3. The senators and representatives before mentioned, and the members of the several State legislatures, and all executive and

judicial officers, both of the United States and of the several States, shall be bound by oath or affirmation to support this Constitution; but no religious test shall ever be required as a qualification to any office or public trust under the United States.

ARTICLE VII

The ratification of the conventions of nine States shall be sufficient for the establishment of this Constitution between the States so ratifying the same.

Done in Convention by the unanimous consent of the States present the seventeenth day of September in the year of our Lord one thousand seven hundred and eighty-seven, and of the independence of the United States of America the twelfth. In witness whereof we have hereunto subscribed our names.

George Washington, President,
and Deputy from Virginia

NEW HAMPSHIRE
John Langdon
Nicholas Gilman

MASSACHUSETTS
Nathaniel Gorham
Rufus King

CONNECTICUT
William Samuel Johnson
Roger Sherman

NEW YORK
Alexander Hamilton

NEW JERSEY
William Livinston
David Brearley
William Paterson
Jonathan Dayton

DELAWARE
George Read
Gunning Bedford, Junior
John Dickinson
Richard Bassett
Jacob Broom

MARYLAND
James McHenry
Daniel of St. Tho. Jenifer
Daniel Carrol

VIRGINIA
John Blair
James Madison, Junior

NORTH CAROLINA
William Blount
Richard Dobbs Spaight
Hugh Williamson

PENNSYLVANIA
  Benjamin Franklin
  Thomas Mifflin
  Robert Morris
  George Clymer
  Thomas Fitzsimons
  Jared Ingersoll
  James Wilson
  Gouverneur Morris

SOUTH CAROLINA
  John Rutledge
  Charles Cotesworth Pinckney
  Charles Pinckney
  Pierce Butler

GEORGIA
  William Few
  Abraham Baldwin

Attest, William Jackson, Secretary

COURTESY NATIONAL PARK SERVICE

The Bill of Rights

1791

"In all the world's history there is nothing to compare
with the pledges of human rights and freedom that have
been worked into our charter of government. . . ."

—IRVING BRANT

*From the time of the Magna Carta to the English Bill of Rights
of 1689, the people had had to carve out their individual rights
from the sovereign powers that dominated them, but, in Philadelphia in 1787, the framers of the Constitution at first believed
that there was no need for them to draw up a bill of rights to
protect the individual, since the central government they were
creating was to have only limited powers from the beginning. At
the Convention there were, however, those who felt the need
for explicit statements that spelled out also what the government
could not do. Jefferson, in Paris, was of the same mind; he expressed deep regret when he learned that the proposed Constitution had no guarantees of individual liberties: "A Bill of Rights,"
he wrote Madison, "is what the people are entitled to against any
government."*

*It was not until the Constitution went to the States for ratifica-
tion that the desire of the people for a bill of rights was made
known. Several States refused to ratify the Constitution without
the firm promise of a bill of rights: after all, it was largely for
such rights that they had fought the Revolution in the first place.*

*As a member of the new House of Representatives, James
Madison, in June 1789, drew up articles guaranteeing certain individual liberties, and these—edited and altered—were finally
passed by the House on September 24, by the Senate on September*

25, 1789. Over two years later—December 15, 1791—the States completed ratification of these articles, which became the first ten Amendments of the Constitution, what President Franklin Roosevelt, at a ceremony celebrating the 150th anniversary of the ratification, called "the great American charter of personal liberty and human dignity."

Although these ten Amendments have traditionally been considered the American Bill of Rights, historian Irving Brant has pointed out that both the original Constitution and later Amendments also include important guarantees of individual rights, as indeed do such documents as the Emancipation Proclamation and the Civil Rights Act of 1965.

But it is those ten Amendments that provide the firm foundation for the liberties that most Americans have long since come to accept—at least in name—as a part of our way of life:—freedom of speech, of the press, and of religion; freedom to assemble peaceably; freedom from search and seizure; the right to a speedy and public trial—those rights that are never honored in a police state, whether it be fascist or communist. Indeed, these are the priceless freedoms that most sharply distinguish the United States of America from the Communist world, the freedoms that are always, to some degree, in danger of being lost. Only seven years after those ten Amendments were ratified, a Federalist Congress passed the Sedition Act, severely restricting freedom of speech and the press. After Jefferson became president, in 1801, the Act was not renewed. But in the years since, extremist groups like the Know-Nothings of the nineteenth century, the KKK, and super-patriot organizations have frequently threatened the liberties and freedoms guaranteed all Americans under the Bill of Rights. These freedoms—the very keystone of a free society—are as fragile as they are valuable. Each American has the privilege of enjoying, and helping to preserve, this rich heritage; each must heed those words carved on the wall of the National Archives in Washington, where the original copy of the Bill of Rights is enshrined: "Eternal vigilance is the price of liberty."

THE NATIONAL ARCHIVES

The Bill of Rights.

ARTICLE I

Congress shall make no law respecting an establishment of religion, or prohibiting the free exercise thereof; or abridging the freedom of speech, or of the press; or the right of the people peaceably to assemble, and to petition the government for a redress of grievances.

ARTICLE II

A well regulated militia being necessary to the security of a free State, the right of the people to keep and bear arms shall not be infringed.

ARTICLE III

No soldier shall, in time of peace, be quartered in any house, without the consent of the owner, nor in time of war, but in a manner to be prescribed by law.

ARTICLE IV

The right of the people to be secure in their persons, houses, papers, and effects, against unreasonable searches and seizures, shall not be violated, and no warrants shall issue, but upon probable cause, supported by oath or affirmation, and particularly describing the place to be searched, and the persons or things to be seized.

ARTICLE V

No person shall be held to answer for a capital, or otherwise infamous crime, unless on a presentment or indictment of a grand jury, except in cases arising in the land or naval forces, or in the militia, when in actual service in time of war or public danger; nor shall any person be subject for the same offense to be twice put in jeopardy of life or limb; nor shall be compelled in any criminal case to be a witness against himself, nor be deprived of life, liberty, or property, without due process of law; nor shall private property be taken for public use without just compensation.

ARTICLE VI

In all criminal prosecutions, the accused shall enjoy the right to a speedy and public trial, by an impartial jury of the State and district wherein the crime shall have been committed, which district shall have been previously ascertained by law, and to be informed of the nature and cause of the accusation; to be confronted with the witnesses against him; to have compulsory process for obtaining witnesses in his favor, and to have the assistance of counsel for his defense.

ARTICLE VII

In suits at common law, where the value in controversy shall exceed twenty dollars, the right of trial by jury shall be preserved, and no fact tried by a jury shall be otherwise reexamined in any court of the United States, than according to the rules of the common law.

ARTICLE VIII

Excessive bail shall not be required, nor excessive fines imposed, nor cruel and unusual punishments inflicted.

ARTICLE IX

The enumeration in the Constitution of certain rights shall not be construed to deny or disparage others retained by the people.

ARTICLE X

The powers not delegated to the United States by the Constitution, nor prohibited by it to the States, are reserved to the States respectively, or to the people.

Additional Amendments

ARTICLE XI

Passed by Congress March 5, 1794   *Ratified January 8, 1798*

The judicial power of the United States shall not be construed to extend to any suit in law or equity, commenced or prosecuted against one of the United States by citizens of another State, or by citizens or subjects of any foreign State.

ARTICLE XII

Passed by Congress December 12, 1803 Ratified September 25, 1804

The electors shall meet in their respective States, and vote by ballot for President and Vice President, one of whom, at least, shall not be an inhabitant of the same State with themselves; they shall name in their ballots the person voted for as President, and in distinct ballots, the person voted for as Vice President, and they shall make distinct lists of all persons voted for as President and of all persons voted for as Vice President, and of the number of votes for each, which lists they shall sign and certify, and transmit sealed to the seat of the government of the United States, directed to the President of the Senate;—The President of the Senate shall, in the presence of the Senate and House of Representatives, open all the certificates and the votes shall then be counted;—The person having the greatest number of votes for President, shall be the President, if such number be a majority of the whole number of electors appointed; and if no person have such majority, then from the persons having the highest numbers not exceeding three on the list of those voted for as President, the House of Representatives shall choose immediately, by ballot, the President. But in choosing the President, the votes shall be taken by States, the representation from each State having one vote; a quorum for this purpose shall consist of a member or members from two-thirds of the States, and a majority of all the States shall be necessary to a choice. And if the House of Representatives shall not choose a President whenever the right of choice shall devolve upon them, before the fourth day of March next following, then the Vice President shall act as President, as in the case of the death or other constitutional disability of the President. The person having the greatest number of votes as Vice President shall be the Vice President, if such number be a majority of the whole number of electors appointed, and if no person have a majority, then from the two highest numbers on the list, the Senate shall choose the Vice President; a quorum for the purpose shall consist of two thirds of the whole number of Senators, and a majority of the whole number shall be necessary to a choice. But no person constitutionally ineligible to the office of President shall be eligible to that of Vice President of the United States.

ARTICLE XIII

Passed by Congress February 1, 1865   Ratified December 18, 1866

Section 1. Neither slavery nor involuntary servitude, except as punishment for crime whereof the party shall have been duly convicted, shall exist within the United States, or any place subject to their jurisdiction.

Section 2. Congress shall have power to enforce this article by appropriate legislation.

ARTICLE XIV

Passed by Congress June 16, 1866   *Ratified July 28, 1868*

Section 1. All persons born or naturalized in the United States, and subject to the jurisdiction thereof, are citizens of the United States and of the State wherein they reside. No State shall make or enforce any law which shall abridge the privileges or immunities of citizens of the United States; nor shall any State deprive any person of life, liberty, or property, without due process of law; nor deny to any person within its jurisdiction the equal protection of the laws.

Section 2. Representatives shall be apportioned among the several States according to their respective numbers, counting the whole number of persons in each State, excluding Indians not taxed. But when the right to vote at any election for the choice of electors for President and Vice President of the United States, representatives in Congress, the executive and judicial officers of a State, or the members of the legislature thereof, is denied to any of the male inhabitants of such State, being twenty-one years of age, and citizens of the United States, or in any way abridged, except for participation in rebellion, or other crime, the basis of representation therein shall be reduced in the proportion which the number of such male citizens shall bear to the whole number of male citizens twenty-one years of age in such State.

Section 3. No person shall be a senator or representative in Congress, or elector of President and Vice President, or hold any office, civil or military, under the United States, or under any State, who having previously taken an oath, as a member of Congress, or as an officer of the United States, or a member of any State legislature, or as an executive or judicial officer of any State, to support the Constitution of the United States, shall have engaged in insurrection or rebellion against the same, or given aid or comfort to the enemies thereof. But Congress may by a vote of two-thirds of each House, remove such disability.

Section 4. The validity of the public debt of the United States, authorized by law, including debts incurred for payment of pensions and bounties for services in suppressing insurrection or rebellion, shall not be questioned. But neither the United States nor any State shall assume or pay any debt or obligation incurred in aid of insurrection or rebellion against the United States, or any claim for the loss or emancipation of any slave; but all such debts, obligations, and claims shall be held illegal and void.

Section 5. The Congress shall have power to enforce, by appropriate legislation, the provisions of this article.

ARTICLE XV

Passed by Congress February 26, 1869   Ratified March 30, 1870

Section 1. The right of citizens of the United States to vote shall not be denied or abridged by the United States or by any State on account of race, color, or previous condition of servitude.

Section 2. The Congress shall have power to enforce this article by appropriate legislation.

ARTICLE XVI

Passed by Congress July 12, 1909   Ratified February 25, 1913

The Congress shall have power to lay and collect taxes on incomes, from whatever source derived, without apportionment among the several States, and without regard to any census or enumeration.

ARTICLE XVII

Passed by Congress May 16, 1912   Ratified May 31, 1913

Section 1. The Senate of the United States shall be composed of two senators from each State, elected by the people thereof, for six years; and each senator shall have one vote. The electors in each

State shall have the qualifications requisite for electors of the most numerous branch of the State legislature.

Section 2. When vacancies happen in the representation of any State in the Senate, the executive authority of such State shall issue writs of election to fill such vacancies: *Provided,* That the legislature of any State may empower the executive thereof to make temporary appointments until the people fill the vacancies by election as the legislature may direct.

Section 3. This amendment shall not be so construed as to affect the election or term of any senator chosen before it becomes valid as part of the Constitution.

ARTICLE XVIII

Passed by Congress December 18, 1917   Ratified January 29, 1919

Section 1. After one year from the ratification of this article, the manufacture, sale, or transportation of intoxicating liquors within, the importation thereof into, or the exportation thereof from the United States and all territory subject to the jurisdiction thereof for beverage purposes is hereby prohibited.

Section 2. The Congress and the several States shall have concurrent power to enforce this article by appropriate legislation.

Section 3. This article shall be inoperative unless it shall have been ratified as an amendment to the Constitution by the legislatures of the several States, as provided in the Constitution, within seven years from the date of the submission hereof to the States by Congress.

ARTICLE XIX

Passed by Congress June 5, 1919   Ratified August 26, 1920

Section 1. The right of citizens of the United States to vote shall not be denied or abridged by the United States or by any State on account of sex.

Section 2. The Congress shall have power by appropriate legislation to enforce the provisions of this article.

ARTICLE XX

Passed by Congress March 3, 1932   Ratified February 6, 1933

Section 1. The terms of the President and Vice President shall end at noon on the 20th day of January, and the terms of Senators and Representatives at noon on the 3d day of January, of the years in which such terms would have ended if this article had not been ratified; and the terms of their successors shall then begin.

Section 2. The Congress shall assemble at least once in every year, and such meeting shall begin at noon on the 3d day of January, unless they shall by law appoint a different day.

Section 3. If, at the time fixed for the beginning of the term of the President, the President-elect shall have died, the Vice President-elect shall become President. If a President shall not have been chosen before the time fixed for the beginning of his term, or if the President-elect shall have failed to qualify, then the Vice President-elect shall act as President until a President shall have qualified; and the Congress may by law provide for the case wherein neither a President-elect nor a Vice President-elect shall have qualified, declaring who shall then act as President, or the manner in which one who is to act shall be selected, and such person shall act accordingly until a President or Vice President shall have qualified.

Section 4. The Congress may by law provide for the case of the death of any of the persons from whom the House of Representatives may choose a President whenever the right of choice shall have devolved upon them, and for the case of the death of any of the persons from whom the Senate may choose a Vice President whenever the right of choice shall have devolved upon them.

Section 5. Sections 1 and 2 shall take effect on the 15th day of October following the ratification of this article.

Section 6. This article shall be inoperative unless it shall have been ratified as an amendment to the Constitution by the legislatures of three-fourths of the several States within seven years from the date of its submission.

ARTICLE XXI

Passed by Congress February 20, 1933 Ratified December 5, 1933

Section 1. The eighteenth article of amendment to the Constitution of the United States is hereby repealed.

Section 2. The transportation or importation into any State, Territory, or possession of the United States for delivery or use therein of intoxicating liquors in violation of the laws thereof, is hereby prohibited.

Section 3. This article shall be inoperative unless it shall have been ratified as an amendment to the Constitution by conventions in the several States, as provided in the Constitution, within seven years from the date of the submission thereof to the States by the Congress.

ARTICLE XXII

Passed by Congress March 12, 1947   Ratified February 26, 1951

Section 1. No person shall be elected to the office of the President more than twice, and no person who has held the office of President, or acted as President, for more than two years of a term to which some other person was elected President shall be elected to the office of the President more than once.

But this article shall not apply to any person holding the office of President when this article was proposed by the Congress, and shall not prevent any person who may be holding the office of President, or acting as President, during the term within which this article becomes operative from holding the office of President or acting as President during the remainder of such term.

Section 2. This article shall be inoperative unless it shall have been ratified as an amendment to the Constitution by the legislatures of three fourths of the several States within seven years from the date of its submission to the States by the Congress.

ARTICLE XXIII

Passed by Congress June 16, 1960   Ratified March 29, 1961

Section 1. The District constituting the seat of Government of the United States shall appoint in such manner as the Congress may direct:

A number of electors of President and Vice President equal to the whole number of Senators and Representatives in Congress to which the District would be entitled if it were a State, but in no event more than the least populous state; they shall be in addition to those appointed by the states, but shall be considered, for the purpose of the election of President and Vice President, to be electors appointed by a State; and they shall meet in the District and perform such duties as provided by the twelfth article of amendment.

Section 2. The Congress shall have power to enforce this article by appropriate legislation.

ARTICLE XXIV

Passed by Congress August 27, 1962   Ratified January 23, 1964

Section 1. The right of citizens of the United States to vote in any primary or other election for President or Vice President, for electors for President or Vice President, or for Senator or Representative in Congress, shall not be denied or abridged by the United States or any State by reason of failure to pay any poll tax or other tax.

Section 2. The Congress shall have the power to enforce this article by appropriate legislation.

ARTICLE XXV

Passed by Congress July 6, 1965   Ratified February 10, 1967

Section 1. In case of the removal of the President from office or his death or resignation, the Vice President shall become President.

Section 2. Whenever there is a vacancy in the office of the Vice President, the President shall nominate a Vice President who shall take the office upon confirmation by a majority vote of both houses of Congress.

Section 3. Whenever the President transmits to the President pro tempore of the Senate and the Speaker of the House of Representatives his written declaration that he is unable to discharge the powers and duties of his office, and until he transmits to them a written declaration to the contrary, such powers and duties shall be discharged by the Vice President as Acting President.

Section 4. Whenever the Vice President and a majority of either the principal officers of the executive departments or of such other body as Congress may by law provide, transmit to the President pro tempore of the Senate and the Speaker of the House of Representatives their written declaration that the President is unable to discharge the powers and duties of his office, the Vice President shall immediately assume the powers and duties of the office as Acting President.

Thereafter, when the President transmits to the President pro tempore of the Senate and the Speaker of the House of Representatives his written declaration that no inability exists, he shall resume the powers and duties of his office unless the Vice President and a majority of either the principal officers of the executive department or of such other body as Congress may by law provide, transmit within four days to the President pro tempore of the Senate and the Speaker of the House of Representatives their written declaration that the President is unable to discharge the powers and duties of his office. Thereupon Congress shall decide the issue, assembling within 48 hours if not in session. If the Congress, within 21 days after receipt of the latter written declaration, or, if Congress is not in session, within 21 days after Congress is required to assemble, determines by two-thirds vote of both houses that the President is unable to discharge the powers and duties of his office, the Vice President shall continue to discharge the same as Acting President; otherwise, the President shall resume the powers and duties of his office.

THE NATIONAL ARCHIVES

Imprint of the Great Seal of the United States.

OLD STATE HOUSE, PHILADELPHIA.

COURTESY THE HISTORICAL SOCIETY OF PENNSYLVANIA

First Inaugural Address
Thomas Jefferson
1801

"By word and deed Jefferson taught his countrymen an unforgettable lesson in the peaceful transfer of authority."
—DUMAS MALONE

The election of 1800 saw the beginnings of political parties in the United States. John Adams had barely won over Thomas Jefferson and his growing Republican Party in 1796. Firmly established under Washington were the Federalists—men who held to the idea of a strong central government. Under Adams, however, the passion of some Federalists to regulate—and to dominate—led to the passage, in 1798, of the Alien and Sedition Acts, acts as oppressive and intolerable to free men as were some of the acts of the British in the 1760s.

The Alien Acts were directed against foreigners, most of whom were sympathetic to the cause of the growing Republican Party. The Acts deprived aliens of some of their rights and extended the naturalization period from five to fourteen years—prolonging the time the newcomer had to wait before he could vote. The Sedition Act gave the Government the power to imprison any citizen who was overly critical of the Government—in effect severely restricting freedom of speech and the press. The Federalists had gone to extremes, and, powerful as they were, they were repudiated at the polls in the election that has sometimes been called the "bloodless revolution"; Jefferson himself called the election "as real a revolution in the principles of our government as that of 1776 was in its form."

Friends & fellow citizens

Called upon to undertake the duties of the first Executive office of our country I avail myself of the presence of that portion of my fellow citizens which is here assembled to express my grateful thanks for the favor with which they have been pleased to look towards me to declare a sincere consciousness that the task is above my talents, & that I approach it with those anxious & awful presentiments which the greatness of the charge & the weakness of my powers so justly inspire. a rising nation, spread over a wide & fruitful land, traversing all the seas with the rich productions of their industry, engaged in commerce with nations who feel power & forget right, advancing rapidly to destinies beyond the reach of mortal eye; when I contemplate these transcendent objects, & see the honour, the happiness, & the hopes of this beloved country, committed to the issue & the auspices of this day, I shrink from the contemplation & humble myself before the magnitude of the undertaking. utterly, indeed should I despair, did not the presence of many, whom I here see, remind me, that in the other high authorities provided by our constitution, I shall find resources of wisdom, of virtue, & of zeal on which to rely, under all difficulties. to you then, gentlemen, who are charged with the sovereign functions of legislation & to those associated with you, I look with encouragement for that guidance & support which may enable us to steer with safety the vessel in which we are all embarked, amidst the conflicting elements of a troubled world.

During the contest of opinion — " — through which we have past, the animation of discussions & of exertions has sometimes worn an aspect which might impose on strangers unused to think freely, & to speak & to write what they think. but this being now decided by the voice of the nation, enounced according to — the rules of the constitution all will of course arrange themselves under the will of the law & unite in common efforts for the common good. the successful majority too will keep in mind this sacred principle that tho' the the will of the majority is in all cases to prevail that will, to be rightful must be reasonable; that the minority possess their equal rights, which equal laws must protect, & to violate would be oppression. let us then fellow citizens, unite with one heart & one mind, let us restore to social intercourse that harmony & affection without which liberty, & even life itself are but dreary things. and let us reflect that having banished from our land that religious intolerance under which mankind so long bled & suffered we have yet gained little if we countenance a political intolerance, as despotic, as wicked, & capable of

LIBRARY OF CONGRESS

First page of Jefferson's First Inaugural Address.

The importance of the bloodless quality of this "revolution" can scarcely be exaggerated: This was the first real test of the newly created government—the first time the power to rule passed from the Federalists into the hands of an opposing political group, and it is a milestone in the history of government precisely because this change was made peaceably. It is perhaps the first time in history that there was such a radical change in the parties in power—without warfare. The Constitution's solution to the age-old problem of succession, which had not really been tested when Adams replaced Washington, had now proved itself: after the election of 1800, the young nation could boast that it had solved the problem of succession, the problem that throughout history had caused—and continues today to cause—strife and bloodshed.

Significantly, Jefferson's inauguration was the first to take place in the nation's new capital on the Potomac. The election had found the parties dangerously far apart, and, in his address, Jefferson took pains to emphasize what united rather than separated them: "We are all republicans—we are all federalists." And, in memorable phrases, he restated the great principles on which this self-governing, free society had been established.

Jefferson knew that this election and the peaceful transfer of power had severely tested the flexibility of the young republic, and he was striving to reduce the strain. Yet, he could not wander from his deeply held principles; in this address he could not refrain from condemning the narrow view represented by the Sedition Act with his great affirmation of the value of freedom of speech:

> If there be any among us who would wish to dissolve this Union or to change its republican form, let them stand undisturbed as monuments of the safety with which error of opinion may be tolerated when reason is left free to combat it.

CALLED UPON to undertake the duties of the first executive office of our country, I avail myself of the presence of that portion of my fellow-citizens which is here assembled to express my grateful thanks for the favor with which they have been pleased to look toward me, to declare a sincere consciousness that the task is above my talents, and that I approach it with those anxious and awful presentiments which the greatness of the charge and the weakness of my powers so justly inspire. A rising nation, spread over a wide and fruitful land, traversing all the seas with the rich productions of their industry, engaged in commerce with nations who feel power and forget right, advancing rapidly to destinies beyond the reach of mortal eye—when I contemplate these transcendent objects, and see the honor, the happiness, and the hopes of this beloved country committed to the issue, and the auspices of this day, I shrink from the contemplation, and humble myself before the magnitude of the undertaking. Utterly, indeed, should I despair did not the presence of many whom I here see remind me that in the other high authorities provided by our Constitution I shall find resources of wisdom, of virtue, and of zeal on which to rely under all difficulties. To you, then, gentlemen, who are charged with the sovereign functions of legislation, and to those associated with you, I look with encouragement for that guidance and support which may enable us to steer with safety the vessel in which we are all embarked amidst the conflicting elements of a troubled world.

During the contest of opinion through which we have passed the animation of discussions and of exertions has sometimes worn an aspect which might impose on strangers unused to think freely and to speak and to write what they think; but this being now decided by the voice of the nation, announced according to the rules of the Constitution, all will of course arrange themselves under the will of the law, and unite in common efforts for the common good. All, too, will bear in mind this sacred principle, that though the will of the majority is in all cases to prevail, that will to be rightful must be reasonable; that the minority possesses their equal rights, which equal law must protect, and to violate would be oppression. Let us, then, fellow-citizens, unite with one heart and one mind. Let us restore to social intercourse that harmony and affection without which liberty and even life itself are but dreary things. And let us reflect that, having banished from our land that religious intolerance under which mankind so long bled and suffered, we have yet gained little if we countenance a political intolerance as despotic, as wicked, and capable of as bitter and bloody persecutions. During the throes and convulsions of the ancient world, during the agonizing spasms of infuriated man, seeking through blood and slaughter his long-lost liberty, it was not wonderful that the agitation of the billows should reach even this distant and peaceful shore; that this should be more felt and feared by some and less by others, and should divide opinions as to measures of safety. But every difference of opinion is not a difference of principle. We have called by different names brethren of the same principle. We are all republicans, we are all federalists. If there be any among us who would wish to dissolve this Union or to change its republican form, let them stand undisturbed as monuments of the safety with which error of opinion may be tolerated where reason is left free to combat it. I know, indeed, that some honest men fear that a republican government can not be strong, that this Government is not strong enough; but would the honest patriot, in the full tide of successful experiment, abandon a government which has so far kept us free and firm on the theoretic and visionary fear that this Government, the world's best hope, may by possibility want energy to preserve itself? I trust not. I believe this, on the contrary, the strongest Government on earth. I believe it the only one where every man, at the call of the law, would fly to the standard of the law, and would meet invasions of the public order as his own personal concern. Sometimes it is said that man can not be trusted with the government of himself. Can he, then, be trusted with the government of others? Or have we found angels in the forms of kings to govern him? Let history answer this question.

Let us, then, with courage and confidence pursue our own Federal and Republican principles, our attachment to union and representative government. Kindly separated by nature and a wide ocean from the exterminating havoc of one quarter of the globe; too high-minded to endure the degradations of the others; possessing a chosen country, with room enough for our descendants to the thousandth and thousandth generation; entertaining a due sense of our equal right to the use of our own faculties, to the acquisitions of our own industry, to honor and confidence from our fellow-citizens, resulting not from birth, but from our actions and their sense of them; enlightened by a benign religion, professed, indeed, and practiced in various forms, yet all of them inculcating honesty, truth, temperance, gratitude, and the love of man; acknowledging and adoring an overruling Providence, which by all its dispensations proves that it delights in the happiness of man here and his greater happiness hereafter—with all these blessings, what more is necessary to make us a happy and a prosperous people? Still one thing more, fellow-citizens—a wise and frugal Government, which shall restrain men from injuring one another, shall leave them otherwise free to regulate their own pursuits of industry and improvement, and shall not take from the mouth of labor the bread it has earned. This is the sum of good government, and this is necessary to close the circle of our felicities.

About to enter, fellow-citizens, on the exercise of duties which comprehend everything dear and valuable to you, it is proper you should understand what I deem the essential principles of our Government, and consequently those which ought to shape its Administration. I will compress them within the narrowest compass they will bear, stating the general principle, but not all its limitations. Equal and exact justice to all men, of whatever state or persuasion, religious or political; peace, commerce, and honest friendship with all nations, entangling alliances with none; the support of the State governments in all their rights, as the most competent administrations for our domestic concerns and the surest bulwarks against antirepublican tendencies; the preservation of the General Government in its whole constitutional vigor, as the sheet anchor of our peace at home and safety abroad; a jealous care of the right of election by the people—a mild and safe corrective of abuses which are lopped by the sword of revolution where peaceable remedies are unprovided; absolute acquiescence in the decisions of the majority, the vital principle of republics, from which is no appeal but to force, the vital principle and immediate parent of despotism; a well-disciplined militia, our best reliance in peace and for the first moments of war, till regulars may relieve them; the supremacy of the civil over the military authority; economy in the public expense, that labor may be lightly burthened; the honest payment of our debts and sacred preservation of the public faith; encouragement of agriculture, and of commerce as its handmaid; the diffusion of information and arraignment of all abuses at the bar of the public reason; freedom of religion; freedom of the press, and freedom of person under the protection of the habeas corpus, and trial by juries impartially selected. These principles form the bright constellation which has gone before us and guided our steps through an age of revolution and reformation. The wisdom of our sages and blood of our heroes have been devoted to their attainment. They should be the creed of our political faith, the text of civic instruction, the touchstone by which to try the services of those we trust; and should we wander from them in moments of error or of alarm, let us hasten to retrace our steps and to regain the road which alone leads to peace, liberty, and safety.

I repair, then, fellow-citizens, to the post you have assigned me. With experience enough in subordinate offices to have seen the difficulties of this the greatest of all, I have learnt to expect that it will rarely fall to the lot of imperfect man to retire from this station with the reputation and the favor which bring him into it. Without pretensions to that high confidence you reposed in our first and greatest revolutionary character, whose preeminent services had entitled him to the first place in his country's love and destined for him the fairest page in the volume of faithful history, I ask so much confidence only as may give firmness and effect to the legal administration of your affairs. I shall often go wrong through defect of judgment. When right, I shall often be thought wrong by those whose positions will not command a view of the whole ground. I ask your indulgence for my own errors, which will never be intentional, and your support against the errors of others, who may condemn what they would not if seen in all its parts. The approbation implied by your suffrage is a great consolation to me for the past, and my future solicitude will be to retain the good opinion of those who have bestowed it in advance, to conciliate that of others by doing them all the good in my power, and to be instrumental to the happiness and freedom of all.

Relying, then, on the patronage of your good will, I advance with obedience to the work, ready to retire from it whenever you become sensible how much better choice it is in your power to make. And may that Infinite Power which rules the destinies of the universe lead our councils to what is best, and give them a favorable issue for your peace and prosperity.

The Emancipation Proclamation

Abraham Lincoln

1863

"I never, in my life, felt more certain that I was doing right, than I do in signing this paper."

—Abraham Lincoln—*on signing the Proclamation*

In his First Inaugural Address, speaking to a nation already torn by secession, President Lincoln had stressed his Constitutional obligation to maintain and defend the Union, not to suppress slavery. And, throughout the first years of the war, he had continued to emphasize the absolute necessity of preserving the Union. The key political issue was not so much slavery itself, but the question of extending slavery into the western territories.

Lincoln was firmly against slavery, but in his First Inaugural he had tried mightily to give the South no provocation. But war had come, and, as it turned into a conflict of frightening proportions, and the cost in life and property mounted, the chief political reason for not proclaiming emancipation vanished—although Lincoln did have doubts about the power of the President to abolish slavery. But in the spring of 1862, after Congress abolished it in the District of Columbia and in the Territories, he was encouraged to begin drafting his Emancipation Proclamation.

Lincoln was against slavery on principle, but he was particularly concerned about slavery in the United States, since he saw it—and especially its expansion—as a direct threat to democracy. But rather than issue a proclamation without warning or notice, Lincoln prepared a Preliminary Emancipation Proclamation, which was issued September 22, 1862. This statement announced that, on January 1,

By the President of the United States of America:

A Proclamation.

Whereas, on the twenty-second day of September, in the year of our Lord one thousand eight hundred and sixty-two, a proclamation was issued by the President of the United States, containing, among other things, the following, to wit:

"That on the first day of January, in the "year of our Lord one thousand eight hundred "and sixty-three, all persons held as slaves within "any State or designated part of a State, the people "whereof shall then be in rebellion against the "United States, shall be then, thenceforward, and "forever free; and the Executive Government of the "United States, including the military and naval "authority thereof, will recognize and maintain "the freedom of such persons, and will do no act "or acts to repress such persons, or any of them, "in any efforts they may make for their actual "freedom.

"That the Executive will, on the first of

First page of the Emancipation Proclamation.

1863, all slaves in States or parts of States then in rebellion would be forever free.

Some Americans doubted that Lincoln would actually issue the Emancipation Proclamation, but he worked carefully in drafting and revising the document that he signed, in his office in the White House, on January 1, 1863. President Lincoln had taken the first mighty step down the long road toward the realization of the American ideal of equality.

WHEREAS, on the twenty-second day of September, in the year of our Lord one thousand eight hundred and sixty-two, a proclamation was issued by the President of the United States, containing, among other things, the following, to wit:

> That on the first day of January, in the year of our Lord one thousand eight hundred and sixty-three, all persons held as slaves within any State, or designated part of a State, the people whereof shall then be in rebellion against the United States, shall be then, thenceforward, and forever free; and the Executive Government of the United States, including the military and naval authority thereof, will recognize and maintain the freedom of such persons, and will do no act or acts to repress such persons, or any of them, in any efforts they may make for their actual freedom.

> That the Executive will, on the first day of January aforesaid, by proclamation, designate the States and parts of States, if any, in which the people thereof respectively shall then be in rebellion against the United States; and the fact that any State, or the people thereof, shall on that day be in good faith represented in the Congress of the United States by members chosen thereto at elections wherein a majority of the qualified voters of such State shall have participated, shall in the absence of strong countervailing testimony be deemed conclusive evidence that such State and the people thereof are not then in rebellion against the United States.

Now, therefore, I, Abraham Lincoln, President of the United States, by virtue of the power in me vested as Commander-in-Chief of the Army and Navy of the United States, in time of actual armed rebellion against the authority and government of the United States, and as a fit and necessary war measure for suppressing said rebellion, do, on this first day of January, in the year of our Lord one thousand eight hundred and sixty-three, and in accordance with my purpose so to do, publicly proclaimed for the full period of 100 days from the day first above mentioned, order and designate as the States and parts of States wherein the people thereof, respectively, are this day in rebellion against the United States, the following, to wit:

> Arkansas, Texas, Louisiana (except the parishes of St. Bernard, Plaquemines, Jefferson, St. John, St. Charles, St. James, Ascension, Assumption, Terre Bonne, Lafourche, St. Mary, St. Martin, and Orleans, including the city of New Orleans), Mississippi, Alabama, Florida, Georgia, South Carolina, North Carolina, and Virginia (except the forty-eight counties designated as West Virginia, and also the counties of Berkeley, Accomac, Northampton, Elizabeth City, York, Princess Anne, and Norfolk, including the cities of Norfolk and Portsmouth), and which excepted parts are for the present left precisely as if this proclamation were not issued.

And by virtue of the power and for the purpose aforesaid, I do order and declare that all persons held as slaves within said designated States and parts of States are, and henceforward shall be, free; and that the Executive Government of the United States, including the military and naval authorities thereof, shall recognize and maintain the freedom of said persons.

And I hereby enjoin upon the people so declared to be free to abstain from all violence, unless in necessary self-defense; and I recommend to them that, in all cases where allowed, they labor faithfully for reasonable wages.

And I further declare and make known that such persons of suitable condition will be received into the armed service of the United States to garrison forts, positions, stations, and other places, and to man vessels of all sorts in said service.

And upon this act, sincerely believed to be an act of justice, warranted by the Constitution upon military necessity, I invoke the considerate judgment of mankind and the gracious favor of Almighty God.

In witness whereof, I have hereunto set my hand and caused the seal of the United States to be affixed.

Done at the city of Washington, the first day of January, in the year of our Lord one thousand eight hundred and sixty-three, and of the independence of the United States of America the eighty-seventh.

By the President:

Abraham Lincoln

William H. Seward, Secretary of State

Lincoln reading the Emancipation Proclamation to his cabinet: *Seated*—Edwin Stanton, Secretary of War; Lincoln; Gideon Welles, Secretary of the Navy; William Seward, Secretary of State; Edward Bates, Attorney General. *Standing*—Salmon Chase, Secretary of the Treasury; Caleb Smith, Secretary of the Interior; and Montgomery Blair, Postmaster General. Painting by Francis Bicknell Carpenter.

COURTESY CAPITOL HISTORICAL SOCIETY

The Gettysburg Address

Abraham Lincoln

1863

"It will be remembered as long as anyone's speeches are remembered who speaks in the English language."

—EDWIN STANTON

The battle fought at Gettysburg, Pennsylvania, in July of 1863 was a terrible contest, with thousands dead on both sides. By repelling the Confederate invasion of the North, the Union forces gained an important victory, one that many historians believe was the turning point of the Civil War. In order that the thousands slain in battle might be properly buried and have a fitting memorial, a special commission set aside a part of the battlefield for a cemetery. The battle had been one of the great trials—and one of the great moments—in American history, and the ceremony dedicating the cemetery on that battlefield was to provide another.

On November 18, 1863, President Lincoln took a special train to Gettysburg. He had been invited there to say "a few appropriate remarks" after the scholar, statesman, and well-known orator Edward Everett delivered the principal address at the ceremony dedicating the cemetery. Lincoln finished drafting his speech that night in Gettysburg; the next afternoon, after Everett had spoken for almost two hours, Lincoln read his address in less than two minutes.

Response to the address was mixed. Some newspapers mocked it: "We pass over the silly remarks of the President . . ." (Harrisburg Patriot and Union); "Mr. Lincoln did most foully traduce the motives of the men who were slain at Gettysburg. . . ." (Chicago Times). But others gave it high praise: "Could the most

Four score and seven years ago our fathers brought forth, upon this continent, a new nation, conceived in Liberty, and dedicated to the proposition that all men are created equal.

Now we are engaged in a great civil war, testing whether that nation, or any nation, so conceived, and so dedicated, can long endure. We are met here on a great battle-field of that war. We have come to dedicate a portion of it as a final resting place for those who here gave their lives that that nation might live. It is altogether fitting and proper that we should do this.

But in a larger sense we can not dedicate— we can not consecrate— we can not hallow this ground. The brave men, living and dead, who struggled here, have consecrated it far above our poor power to add or detract. The world will little note, nor long remember, what we say here, but can never forget what they did here. It is for us, the living, rather to be dedicated here to the unfinished work which they have, thus far, so nobly carried on. It is rather

LIBRARY OF CONGRESS

The Gettysburg Address, second draft.

elaborate and splendid oration be more beautiful, more touching, more inspiring than those thrilling words of the President? They had in our humble judgment the charm and power of the very highest eloquence" (Providence Journal). *"The dedicatory remarks of President Lincoln will live among the annals of man"* (Chicago Tribune). *And Edward Everett wrote Lincoln: "Permit me . . . to express my great admiration for the thoughts expressed by you, with such eloquent simplicity and appropriateness, at the consecration of the cemetery. I should be glad, if I could flatter myself, that I came as near to the central idea of the occasion in two hours, as you did in two minutes."*

Lincoln had indeed come "near to the central idea": he had put the battle—and the entire war—in its largest possible context, referring, in his first sentence, to that document full of radical ideas that had started this dangerous experiment in free government. The war—and that battle—were keeping that experiment alive, and some of the greatness of Lincoln's address derives from his seeing that terrible battle in its fullest significance—in giving honest meaning and noble purpose to the slaughter, and, at the same time, in seeing this harsh battle for no more than it was—only one step in the very demanding, continuous process of making a free government a reality. No American reading the Gettysburg Address can miss Lincoln's message—his emphasis on continuity, on challenge, and on sacrifice and devotion: by acknowledging the supremacy of what the soldiers did, he touched the very nerve of democracy and free government. And he saw the outcome of the battle as no golden victory, but as an opportunity, purchased at great human cost, for the living, in their turn, to resolve to do—simply to do their part to continue to keep the experiment in free government alive.

☆ ☆ ☆

FOURSCORE AND SEVEN years ago our fathers brought forth on this continent a new nation, conceived in liberty, and dedicated to the proposition that all men are created equal.

Now we are engaged in a great civil war, testing whether that nation, or any nation so conceived and so dedicated, can long endure. We are met on a great battlefield of that war. We have come to dedicate a portion of that field as a final resting-place for those who here gave their lives that that nation might live. It is altogether fitting and proper that we should do this.

But, in a larger sense, we cannot dedicate—we cannot consecrate—we cannot hallow—this ground. The brave men, living and dead, who struggled here, have consecrated it far above our poor power to add or detract. The world will little note nor long remember what we say here, but it can never forget what they did here. It is for us, the living, rather, to be dedicated here to the unfinished work which they who fought here have thus far so nobly advanced. It is rather for us to be here dedicated to the great task remaining before us—that from these honored dead we take increased devotion to that cause for which they gave the last full measure of devotion; that we here highly resolve that these dead shall not have died in vain; that this nation, under God, shall have a new birth of freedom; and that government of the people, by the people, for the people, shall not perish from the earth.

Second Inaugural Address
Abraham Lincoln
1865

"This Inaugural strikes me in its grand simplicity and directness as being for all time the historical keynote of this war. . . ."

—CHARLES FRANCIS ADAMS, JR.

In March of 1865 the outcome of the Civil War was certain: it was simply a matter of time. But the war was still the dominant fact of national life, and it was inevitable that President Lincoln would say something about the prolonged conflict in his Second Inaugural Address. Fourteen months earlier, at Gettysburg, he had given the world his idea of the purpose—and the lesson—of the war, and many Americans wondered what more he could say about it. Certainly few could have anticipated such a brief, soul-searching address, with the President cutting right to the core of the morality of the conflict, and then closing with the magnanimous statement, "With malice toward none . . ."—the great and generous promise to the vanquished that this most unusual of leaders was not destined to live to keep.

AT THIS SECOND appearing to take the oath of the Presidential office there is less occasion for an extended address than there was at the first. Then a statement somewhat in detail of a course to be pursued seemed fitting and proper. Now, at the expiration of four years, during which public declarations have been con-

At this second appearing to take the oath of the presidential office, there is less occasion for an extended address than there was at the first. Then a statement, somewhat in detail, of a course to be pursued, seemed fitting and proper. Now, at the expiration of four years, during which public declarations have been constantly called forth on every point and phase of the great contest which still absorbs the attention, and engrosses the energies of the nation, little that is new could be presented. The progress of our arms, upon which all else chiefly depends, is as well known to the public as to myself; and it is, I trust, reasonably satisfactory and encouraging to all. With high hope for the future, no prediction in regard to it is ventured.

On the occasion corresponding to this four years ago, all thoughts were anxiously directed to an impending civil war. All dreaded it— all sought to avert it. While the inaugeral address was being delivered from this place, devoted altogether to saving the Union without war, in surgents agents were in

LIBRARY OF CONGRESS

First page of Lincoln's Second Inaugural Address.

stantly called forth on every point and phase of the great contest which still absorbs the attention and engrosses the energies of the nation, little that is new could be presented. The progress of our arms, upon which all else chiefly depends, is as well known to the public as to myself, and it is, I trust, reasonably satisfactory and encouraging to all. With high hope for the future, no prediction in regard to it is ventured.

On the occasion corresponding to this four years ago all thoughts were anxiously directed to an impending civil war. All dreaded it, all sought to avert it. While the inaugural address was being delivered from this place, devoted altogether to *saving* the Union without war, insurgent agents were in the city seeking to *destroy* it without war—seeking to dissolve the Union and divide effects by negotiation. Both parties deprecated war, but one of them would *make* war rather than let the nation survive, and the other would *accept* war rather than let it perish, and the war came.

Qne-eighth of the whole population were colored slaves, not distributed generally over the Union, but localized in the southern part of it. These slaves constituted a peculiar and powerful interest. All knew that this interest was somehow the cause of the war. To strengthen, perpetuate, and extend this interest was the object for which the insurgents would rend the Union, even by war; while the Government claimed no right to do more than to restrict the territorial enlargement of it. Neither party expected for the war the magnitude or the duration which it has already attained. Neither anticipated that the *cause* of the conflict might cease with, or even before, the conflict itself should cease. Each looked for an easier triumph, and a result less fundamental and astounding. Both read the same Bible and pray to the same God, and each invokes His aid against the other. It may seem strange that any men should dare to ask a just God's assistance in wringing their bread from the sweat of other men's faces, but let us judge not, that we be not judged. The prayers of both could not be answered. That of neither has been answered fully. The Almighty has His own purposes. "Woe unto the world because of offenses; for it must needs be that offenses come, but woe to

---

LIBRARY OF CONGRESS

President Lincoln delivering his Second Inaugural Address, March 4, 1865.

that man by whom the offense cometh." If we shall suppose that American slavery is one of those offenses which, in the providence of God, must needs come, but which, having continued through His appointed time, He now wills to remove, and that He gives to both North and South this terrible war as the woe due to those by whom the offense came, shall we discern therein any departure from those divine attributes which the believers in a living God always ascribe to Him? Fondly do we hope, fervently do we pray, that this mighty scourge of war may speedily pass away. Yet, if God wills that it continue until all the wealth piled by the bondsman's two hundred and fifty years of unrequited toil shall be sunk, and until every drop of blood drawn with the lash shall be paid by another drawn with the sword, as was said three thousand years ago, so still it must be said "the judgments of the Lord are true and righteous altogether."

With malice toward none, with charity for all, with firmness in the right as God gives us to see the right, let us strive on to finish the work we are in, to bind up the nation's wounds, to care for him who shall have borne the battle and for his widow and his orphan—to do all which may achieve and cherish a just and lasting peace among ourselves and with all nations.

Inaugural Address
John F. Kennedy
1961

"The Inaugural Address of President Kennedy is a manner of summons to citizens by the new head of our great Republic. Around nearly every sentence of it could be written a thesis, so packed is it with implications."

—CARL SANDBURG

"The world is very different now. For man holds in his mortal hands the power to abolish all forms of human poverty and all forms of human life." With these words, President John F. Kennedy put into sharp focus the great challenge of America in the middle of the twentieth century.

Few American Presidents were more serious students of history than President Kennedy; few had his literary talents. And the historian and writer, under the pressure of the dramatic moment of the beginning of his administration, brought forth an address that for both substance and style may well take its place as one of the great American documents of the twentieth century.

Nature conspired to add drama to President Kennedy's inauguration. The night before, a blizzard descended upon Washington, and the Capitol Plaza was cleared only shortly before the ceremony. Against the backdrop of mountains of snow, on a cold, blustery day, President Kennedy delivered his short address with vigor and force. The image of the young President almost shouting his polished phrases into the cold air stirred the shivering thousands at the Plaza and the millions who watched on television. His vibrant presence affirmed that the torch had been "passed to a new generation of Americans".

The address he delivered was lucid and compact with many balanced, pithy statements. And it had more: echoes of Lincoln's great utterances, an organic sense of history and of the Republic, and a tone of urgency and of command heightened by rich figurative language—"Now the trumpet summons us again . . . to bear the burden of a long twilight struggle."

Like Lincoln in his address at Gettysburg, President Kennedy began by referring back to the touchstone of our democracy, the "revolutionary beliefs for which our forebears fought," and he closed with an appeal to his countrymen to help make free government work, to "assure a more fruitful life for all mankind."

The address was a striking success. Its spirit and style appealed to the public and the press; its idealism caught the imagination of many Americans. A number of his phrases—besides the famous, "Ask not what your country can do for you . . ."—were widely quoted: ". . . We shall pay any price, bear any burden, meet any hardship, support any friend, oppose any foe to assure the survival of liberty. . . ." "The energy, the faith, the devotion which we bring to this endeavor will light our country and all who serve it—and the glow from that fire can truly light the world." And the terribly prophetic, "All this will not be finished in the first one hundred days. Nor will it be finished in the first one thousand days, nor in the life of this Administration. . . . But let us begin."

President Kennedy delivering his Inaugural Address, January 20, 1961.

WE OBSERVE TODAY not a victory of party, but a celebration of freedom—symbolizing an end, as well as a beginning—signifying renewal, as well as change. For I have sworn before you and Almighty God the same solemn oath our forebears prescribed nearly a century and three quarters ago.

The world is very different now. For man holds in his mortal hands the power to abolish all forms of human poverty and all forms of human life. And yet the same revolutionary beliefs for which our forebears fought are still at issue around the globe—the belief that the rights of man come not from the generosity of the state, but from the hand of God.

We dare not forget today that we are the heirs of that first revolution. Let the word go forth from this time and place, to friend and foe alike, that the torch has been passed to a new generation of Americans—born in this century, tempered by war, disciplined by a hard and bitter peace, proud of our ancient heritage—and unwilling to witness or permit the slow undoing of those human rights to which this Nation has always been committed, and to which we are committed today at home and around the world.

Let every nation know, whether it wishes us well or ill, that we shall pay any price, bear any burden, meet any hardship, support any friend, oppose any foe, in order to assure the survival and the success of liberty.

This much we pledge—and more.

To those old allies whose cultural and spiritual origins we share, we pledge the loyalty of faithful friends. United, there is little we cannot do in a host of cooperative ventures. Divided, there is little we can do—for we dare not meet a powerful challenge at odds and split asunder.

To those new States whom we welcome to the ranks of the free, we pledge our word that one form of colonial control shall not have passed away merely to be replaced by a far greater iron tyranny. We shall not always expect to find them supporting our view. But we shall always hope to find them strongly supporting their own freedom—and to remember that, in the past, those who foolishly sought power by riding the back of the tiger ended up inside.

To those peoples in the huts and villages across the globe struggling to break the bonds of mass misery, we pledge our best efforts to help them help themselves, for whatever period is required—not because the Communists may be doing it, not because we seek their votes, but because it is right. If a free society cannot help the many who are poor, it cannot save the few who are rich.

To our sister republics south of our border, we offer a special pledge—to convert our good words into good deeds, in a new alliance for progress, to assist free men and free governments in casting off the chains of poverty. But this peaceful revolution of hope cannot become the prey of hostile powers. Let all our neighbors know that we shall join with them to oppose aggression or subversion anywhere in the Americas. And let every other power know that this hemisphere intends to remain the master of its own house.

To that world assembly of sovereign states, the United Nations, our last best hope in an age where the instruments of war have far outpaced the instruments of peace, we renew our pledge of support—to prevent it from becoming merely a forum for invective—to strengthen its shield of the new and the weak—and to enlarge the area in which its writ may run.

Finally, to those nations who would make themselves our adversary, we offer not a pledge but a request: that both sides begin anew the quest for peace, before the dark powers of destruction unleashed by science engulf all humanity in planned or accidental self-destruction.

We dare not tempt them with weakness. For only when our arms are sufficient beyond doubt can we be certain beyond doubt that they will never be employed.

But neither can two great and powerful groups of nations take comfort from our present course—both sides overburdened by the cost of modern weapons, both rightly alarmed by the steady spread of the deadly atom, yet both racing to alter that uncertain balance of terror that stays the hand of mankind's final war.

So let us begin anew—remembering on both sides that civility is not a sign of weakness, and sincerity is always subject to proof. Let us never negotiate out of fear. But let us never fear to negotiate.

Let both sides explore what problems unite us instead of laboring those problems which divide us.

Let both sides, for the first time, formulate serious and precise proposals for the inspection and control of arms—and bring the absolute power to destroy other nations under the absolute control of all nations.

Let both sides seek to invoke the wonders of science instead of its terrors. Together let us explore the stars, conquer the deserts, eradicate disease, tap the ocean depths, and encourage the arts and commerce.

Let both sides unite to heed in all corners of the earth the command of Isaiah—to "undo the heavy burdens and to let the oppressed go free."

And if a beachhead of cooperation may push back the jungle of suspicion, let both sides join in creating a new endeavor, not a new balance of power, but a new world of law, where the strong are just and the weak secure and the peace preserved.

All this will not be finished in the first 100 days. Nor will it be finished in the first 1,000 days, nor in the life of this Administration, nor even perhaps in our lifetime on this planet. But let us begin.

In your hands, my fellow citizens, more than in mine, will rest the final success or failure of our course. Since this country was founded, each generation of Americans has been summoned to give testimony to its national loyalty. The graves of young Americans who answered the call to service surround the globe.

Now the trumpet summons us again—not as a call to bear arms, though arms we need; not as a call to battle, though embattled we are; but a call to bear the burden of a long twilight struggle, year in, and year out, "rejoicing in hope, patient in tribulation"—a struggle against the common enemies of man: tyranny, poverty, disease, and war itself.

Can we forge against these enemies a grand and global alliance, North and South, East and West, that can assure a more fruitful life for all mankind? Will you join in that historic effort?

In the long history of the world, only a few generations have been granted the role of defending freedom in its hour of maximum danger. I do not shrink from this responsibility— I welcome it. I do not believe that any of us would exchange places with any other people or any other generation. The energy, the faith, the devotion which we bring to this endeavor will light our country and all who serve it—and the glow from that fire can truly light the world.

86

And so, my fellow Americans, ask not what your country can do for you: Ask what you can do for your country.

My fellow citizens of the world: Ask not what America will do for you, but what together we can do for the freedom of man.

Finally, whether you are citizens of America or citizens of the world, ask of us the same high standards of strength and sacrifice which we ask of you. With a good conscience our only sure reward, with history the final judge of our deeds, let us go forth to lead the land we love, asking His blessing and His help, but knowing that here on earth God's work must truly be our own.

ACKNOWLEDGEMENTS

The author gratefully acknowledges his indebtedness to the individuals and organizations who made available the illustrations used in this book:

Mr. John D. Kilbourne, The Historical Society of Pennsylvania

The Library of Congress

Mrs. Mary Walton Livingston, The National Archives

Mrs. Florence Miller, The Capitol Historical Society

Mr. James R. Sullivan, Independence National Historical Park, National Park Service

Mrs. Florian H. Thayn, Capitol Architect's Office, The U.S. Capitol

For assistance and advice, the author is indebted to

Mr. Erwin C. Fishel of Arlington, Virginia

Dr. Robert F. Brockmann of the University of Maryland

Miss Liza J. Wilson of the Sandy Spring Friends School, Sandy Spring, Maryland

Mr. Barney Friedland, Mrs. Delia Pierson, Mr. James Sisk, and Mr. James Small of Judd & Detweiler, Inc.

For assistance in preparing material for publication, he is indebted to Mrs. Brenda Smith of Glen Burnie, Maryland.

ABOUT THE AUTHOR

A writer and editor, Mr. Wilson teaches at the University of Maryland. He studied at Cleveland's University School, and at Georgetown, Arizona State, Claremont and Harvard. He is the author of *The Book of the Presidents*.